SUNNY SIDE UP

The 21st century hits a Spanish village

DAVID BAIRD

S

SANTANA BOOKS

First published in May 2004

Copyright ©David Baird 2004.
The Author asserts the moral rights to be
identified as the author of this work.

Designed by Andrea Carter.
Photography by the author.

Sunny Side Up
is published by Ediciones Santana S.L.,
Apartado 422, Fuengirola 29640 (Málaga), Spain.
Tel. 952 485 838. Fax 952 485 367.
E-mail: info@santanabooks.com
www.santanabooks.com

Printed in Spain by Gráficas San Pancracio S.L.,

Depósito Legal: MA-589/2004
ISBN 84-89954-36-4

To Thea

But also to Pura, Antonio, Carmen, Ana, Sebastián, Baldomero, Eduarda, Fernando, Encarna, Rosario, Dolores, Estrella, Paco, María, Rosenda, Pepe, Brígida, Aurelia, Gracia... and all the other neighbours who made us welcome on the Street of Bitterness.

CONTENTS

PROLOGUE

Sometimes I dream about *garbanzos*. Yes, chick-peas, those little bullet-like beans which have to be soaked for days and boiled for hours so that finally you can add some flavouring and create a fine stew, fine that is if you like bullet-like beans.

In the early days, that's what we lived on most of the time, plus a few sardines and plenty of potatoes and tomatoes. Healthy stuff. Better than all that expensive junk in cans. When we first moved into the *pueblo*, we had all we needed. We weren't looking for fancy living, none of urban man's frills and follies. We could do without that. We just wanted a basic back-to-nature existence in the sunshine. The simple life.

It seems a long time ago now. And it is. More than 30 years have gone by. But I can still remember how spartan our existence was. The house had hardly any doors or windows. There was only one cold water tap and the toilet was a hole at the back of the mule's stable. It didn't matter that walking from one side of the room to the other was like taking a ride on a roller coaster. Sloping floors and leaking roofs were part of the fun. Part of the simple life.

Thank heavens for not having a telephone. That meant no wrong numbers, no nerve-jangling midnight calls, no link with the hectic outside world. Television was out, too. What a relief not to be bombarded with commercial jingles and what joy to boast that we hadn't seen a soap opera in years.

"What a way to live!" muttered one visitor from the city, pale and jaded as those types tend to be. "Here you are, perched on a cliff miles from anywhere. No train service, hardly any buses, animals wandering past the door. You need a cable car to reach your house and it's so old it could fall down any moment. No decent Sunday papers. No cinema and precious few shops. The people don't speak a word of English. You live on oranges and fresh air. Good heavens, this village isn't in the 20th century yet."

He was right, of course, absolutely right. Yes, I reflected at the time, a man would be a fool to give all this up.

Best of all was the tranquillity. No pressures, no deadlines. All day to savour ordinary things. All right, conversation in the local bars was not exactly sparkling. A bit heavy on potato prices and somewhat light on intellectual repartee, but who needs smart talk when you're committed to the simple life?

Indeed, life was so good that we used to spend hours just sitting around, chewing our garbanzos, chuckling away at our good fortune and gloating about the miserable time the rest of the world must be having. Just imagining those traffic jams and rain-sodden commuter crowds used to create a warm feeling inside. We were locked into another age and it felt great.

Then the rot set in. One day my wife came home and said: "Do you know what the funny noise is, the one we couldn't figure out? It's Encarna's automatic washing machine."

It was the first blow. Soon afterwards, I noticed a neighbour hauling an outsize television set up the street. The whole village seemed to be on a spending spree. Everybody was acquiring flush toilets and costly gas stoves. Centuries-old beamed roofs and mud walls were being ripped down to make way for marble floors, gaudy floor-to-ceiling tiles and rooftop wash-houses. Whitewash was out, to be covered up where possible by flowery wallpaper. Our simple rustic furniture was swiftly becoming a laughing stock as the neighbours shoehorned colossal veneered sideboards and shiny mock-leather arm-chairs into tiny living rooms. Suddenly, we realised that we had the most primitive house in the street.

The revolution was rolling right up to our ancient, nail-studded (handmade nails, of course) front door. Conspicuous consumption was swamping the *pueblo*. The simple life? Forget it. We were fighting a rearguard action.

The very things that we had fled were taking over here too, and the things that had attracted us were under threat. It was enough to make you weep. We liked the *pueblo* the way it was, the old *pueblo* with its slow gracious ways and a life style embalmed and preserved like a fly in amber. "A land bottled for antiquarians" was the way Richard Ford described Spain back in the 19th century and that is how generations of travellers liked to view it, encouraged by all the romantically inclined visitors from Washington Irving on.

The old ways had such charm. The slow-moving, unchanging rural pattern of life enthralled refugees from the headlong rush of the modern era, with its obsessive pursuit of material gain. Here, in contrast, traditional values held sway. Here there was a sanity and simplicity that had been lost in the so-called sophisticated society of modern Europe. Or that's the way it had seemed to us when we first arrived.

When we found ourselves being dragged once again into the 20th century, we were appalled. It was a shock to realise that most of the *pueblo* was all in favour. Strangely enough, local housewives loved the idea of cooking on electric stoves instead of bending over smoky wood fires; oddly enough the men enjoyed having hot showers after work instead of a brisk rubdown in a corner of the mule's stable, and (how bizarre can one get?) youngsters spurned the quaintness of age-hallowed family homes in favour of airy apartments with gleaming new cars parked outside.

We had been living in a fool's paradise of course. The locals had not been clinging to centuries-old ways because they loved them but because they had no choice. We had mistaken resilience in the face of poverty for picturesque medieval charm. And there was an additional factor. When we first climbed the steps of Calle Amargura, the Street of Bitterness, we knew nothing of the *pueblo*'s recent history, of the dark years that had followed Spain's Civil War when these sierras were bathed in blood. The tranquillity of the *pueblo* did not stem from an easy-going contentment. It was the silence of shattered families, broken hearts and crushed spirit.

Romantic innocents that we were when we set out to enjoy the "simple life", we had little idea of the society into which we were plunging. Thankfully, our new neighbours smothered their astonishment at the ways of these visitors from another planet and with amazing patience and tolerance set about teaching us the complexities of village life. Having knocked about the world a little, we thought we knew a thing or two. We didn't realise that our education was just beginning.

1

COMING TO THE *PUEBLO*

It was the flower that did it. The old lady looked a thousand years old in her widow's weeds. But her eyes were bright and lively. She saw us inspecting the house next to hers and materialised in the doorway to thrust the pink, freshly-picked carnation into Thea's hands. From that moment I knew that the decision was out of my hands.

Perhaps we had known somewhere deep inside that we would end up in the *pueblo* one day. But the route had been a roundabout one. We had first glimpsed it in the mid-1960s. On a brilliant January day, we had walked up the dry river-bed winding inland from the coast, then climbed the valley side in search of a path.

A teenager working in a terraced field shot eager glances at Thea and offered to accompany us. He took Thea by the hand and hurried her along a rocky path up to a cluster of dwellings sprawled over a ridge, the *pueblo*, poor, isolated and forgotten like hundreds of other villages dotted about the sierras of Spain. Finally realising that I was not to be shaken off, the young Don Juan surrendered us to a bunch of children whose numbers increased as we penetrated the narrow streets. Old-timers gaped at us from doorways while the curious children marched behind us, giggling and chattering.

We strolled about the narrow cobbled streets, halted for a drink in what seemed to be the only bar in town and then returned down the valley to the coastal town where we had taken refuge from the English winter while awaiting news of the immigrant vessel that would carry us to Australia.

Five years later we came back. As I had eaten bulldust for breakfast en route to Alice Springs and defended myself from sharp Chinese elbows in crowded Hong Kong lifts, and lived on borsch for seven days and nights on the Trans-Siberian Express, one thought had sustained me. Back in Spain a charming, easygoing place in the sun was awaiting me. A place to escape from crowds, soulless apartment blocks, noise, traffic jams, grasping landlords, money-mad wheeler-dealers, a place where the biggest event of the day was the sun rising in golden glory over the Mediterranean, a place where you could finally unpack the bags and put your feet up.

We planned to buy a place in the coastal resort where we had spent an idyllic winter. Then we saw what they had done to "our town." No sooner had we turned our backs than they had gone absolutely bonkers. Crassest neon glared from every shopfront, cars hooted impatiently on the streets that had known only the tread of goats and donkeys, whole new suburbs had mushroomed dwarfing the old town. In a tourist-packed bar we searched for the cheerful face of the owner, a rascally Civil War veteran who briefly had been our friend. But he was too busy to speak to us. He was counting his takings—and scowling. Tears trickled down my wife's face. Our dream, steeped in nostalgia and romanticism, was shattered.

We tried to come to terms with the situation. We were shown tumbledown fishermen's cottages and asked astronomical prices. We were shown over sterile apartment blocks where the salesman told us, as though to clinch the deal, that the other purchasers were doctors and lawyers from Stuttgart or Toronto. The sales patter convinced us: we had to look elsewhere. After three years in the Hong Kong ant-heap we had not come to Andalusia to live in another apartment block, least of all one that was largely occupied by foreigners. We wanted to live in "Spain."

There was only one way to go. We had to get away from the coast. We took the road to the sierras, and the *pueblo*. Years had gone by since our first visit but, at least on the surface, nothing had changed here. The village straddled a ridge, looking down on a mosaic of intensely-cultivated fields and backed by bleak mountains, which loomed like cardboard Matterhorns against a sky of unreal astonishing blue. Gilded by the autumn light, the flock of interlocking cubist dwellings huddled closely around the old church, as though seeking protection. The whole place breathed permanence and cosy security.

Our contact, who acted as middleman in property deals but in real life delivered bottled gas to the village, led us with amazing agility up what looked like the South face of the Eiger. We could not know that soon it was going to be our street.

Black-clad women gazed at us from their doorways and discussed what could be our business. They knew soon enough. Dolores, a widow, proudly showed off her home. It was a house like none other we had ever seen, a structure that had evolved over centuries, without any tampering from architects. It was like a gingerbread house from a children's fairy tale, except that it grew from the rock. The uneven walls, nearly a metre thick, were built of mud and boulders and held together by countless applications of whitewash.

There were no internal doors; one room simply flowed from another. Here and there the floors sagged as the beams bent with age and rot. The few, shuttered windows were tiny and glassless. Steps, none the same height, led in all directions. The kitchen was dark, with a single cold-water tap and a basin that served both for washing and doing the laundry. Dolores had to bend her ancient back to cook on a wood-fire in the hearth. The bedroom was shared by herself and her son.

"He's going to get married and move to a new house," said Dolores. "So we have to sell this one."

But you could see she did not really want to sell it.

There was an overgrown garden with a fig tree and a grapevine. There was also the view. We stepped through a crumbling door on to the sloping, whitewashed terrace, and gasped. Tiled rooftops fell away dizzyingly to the patchwork fields and beyond to the Mediterranean, a silver-blue shimmer in the autumn sunshine.

Only one thing seemed to be missing and we hesitated to ask, but finally we put the question.

"Follow me," said Dolores, and led us out into the street, then through a door into the mule's stable. Beyond the stable with its food trough and accumulated litter was a small room and in one corner a round hole in the concrete floor. Dolores pointed to the hole with a hint of pride. However the neighbours might manage, her house had its own toilet. A nasty odour came from the hole. This, we learned, gave access to an irrigation channel. Every few days water came plunging down the channel, flushing all debris off to some undisclosed—and better not known—destination down the valley.

It was plain to me that this was not the house we were looking for. This house would be uncomfortable and unpractical and would cost a fortune to modernise. The roof needed repair, the worm-eaten beams needed replacing. Every stick of furniture, every item of food would have to be carted up the street on somebody's back—probably mine. Nobody would want to visit us here. We would be cut off from the world. So deep was the dip in the floor of one room that you needed climbing ropes to cross it. I knocked my head on entering every room. There was no bathroom, no real plumbing. No, this was definitely not the house for us. Anybody could see that.

Then Pura appeared. She smiled, a smile of infinite serenity that lit up her kindly, lined features, as she pressed a flower into Thea's hand and said: "For our new neighbour."

We were lost. We looked at a couple more houses, but they did not have the same character nor the view. Nor did they have Pura. As we took a coffee in the Casino bar, the landlord offered to keep the carnation in water until we left.

"This is a nice village," said my wife.

The haggling took weeks. Details had to be checked with the land registry. As with most of the village houses, there was no escritura (title deed). The house had changed hands several times in the past century, but to avoid taxes the changes had never been officially notified so a new deed had to be prepared. We met in the middleman's house and talked and drank wine and talked some more. The price was 300,000 pesetas, about £1,700 at the current exchange rate and just about our limit. Finally, on the kitchen table beneath a 10-watt bulb, the widow and her sons gathered for the signing of the contract. When it came to Dolores's turn to sign, the middleman carefully inked her thumb with a ballpoint pen and she solemnly made her mark.

"Now my husband is dead and my sons are settled, I've nothing to live for," sighed Dolores. "I'm ready to die, if God wills it."

Two days before we were to receive the key we called on her to see how things were going. She looked surprised to see us but welcomed us in. The pictures were still on the walls. The sparse furniture was in its usual place. There was no sign of any packing.

Tentatively we inquired when we could start moving in. It emerged that the family's purchase of a new house had been held up by lack of cash.

"But"... we stuttered, "we plan to move in on the first of the month. This is our house now. We've nowhere else to go."

"Well, there's room. You can sleep in the upstairs room while I and Manolo have the bedroom downstairs," said Dolores obligingly.

It did not sound the best of arrangements. There was, however, a solution, explained the family. We could make the rest of our payment in advance of occupancy and they could then go ahead with their own purchase. It appeared the only thing to do. But, when the middleman heard what we had done, he was aghast.

"Paid them—and you don't have the key? You should have done it through me."

"But what are you afraid of?" I asked. "Do you think that, now they have the money, they may stay on."

He nodded his head, hopelessly.

"You'll never get them out."

On March 1 we climbed up the Eiger again, debating what we could do if Dolores were still there. You could not throw a 70-year-old widow into the street. The family would not allow it, the *pueblo* would never forgive us. But Dolores was gone, and all her belongings. The mule was gone too, and the stable cleaned out. The house was ours.

We laid a mattress on the sloping floor and bought a chamber pot. We cooked our first supper on a camping stove and told ourselves how tranquil it all was. No sound of motor traffic nor urban bustle. Just the breeze rustling the olive trees. Just piercing children's cries as they raced up and down the stairs next door. Just a couple quarrelling a few houses away. Just two drunks staggering up the street, arguing and cursing and bouncing off the walls.

I could hear somebody snoring. From somewhere came the hoarse, grinding lament of a donkey. A scampering sound suggested there was animal life in the stable. Those thick walls were not the noise-mufflers we had thought. And, even with a foam mattress, the floor was hard.

We couldn't get to sleep. But we didn't mind. We had our own house for the first time. We were *pueblo*-dwellers.

2

LIFE IN THE BARRIO ALTO

Hoofbeats were our alarm clock. They started even before dawn. Men came pacing down the street with their mules, urging them on to the fields.

"*Ay, mula! Mula!*"

The hooves clashed and echoed on the rough cobbles so that they seemed to be thumping right through our living room. In fact, seeing a mule walk out of one of our neighbour's front doors was nothing out of the ordinary. Many were lodged in stables at the back of the dwellings and each morning an esparto mat would be laid across the living room tiles so that they could walk through to the street.

Later came other familiar sounds. Our sturdy neighbour Ana splashed water on the street and there was the soft swish of her brush. A loud squawking, followed by a strangled whimper, indicated that Encarna had started executing chickens for the *pueblo's* lunch table. Another neighbour's clear, untrained voice floated down from a terrace where she sang as she hung out the washing.

"Mizzy, mizzy, mizzy!" called Pura, offering food to the stray cats that prowled over back-gardens and rooftops. Even cat language was different in the *pueblo*.

Raised voices and cackles of laughter signalled the arrival in the Barrio Alto (the upper quarter) of the three rival bakers. They delivered the fresh crusty bread baked in wood ovens to your door, carrying it up the street packed in esparto panniers on the backs of their mules. A little later there might come the trilling melody of the knife-sharpener, blowing his Pipes of Pan. He pushed his ancient motor-cycle up the street and kicked it into life to activate his grinding wheel, which was mounted at the back.

Then came Aurelio, the lottery-ticket seller, tapping the cobbles with his white stick.

"*Qué números tan bonitos!* What pretty numbers!" he bellowed. "Oh, what beautiful numbers I have. Your last chance! Ay, what numbers!"

He was blind, like most ticket-sellers. They had the lottery concession so that they were ensured a livelihood. It was uncanny the way Aurelio could find his way about the *pueblo*, tap-tapping up the steep streets, tap-tapping into the bars. Then, when he had sold all he could, he would park his stick, hop on his motor-cycle, adjust his dark glasses and roar off to the coast.

Aurelio possessed a strong voice, but he could not match the fish-vendors' performance. The two of them came up from the coast every morning and competed fiercely for business as they pushed their barrows along the main street. They were thickset types, wider than they were tall, and their massive chests sheltered lungs of impressive power.

"*Hay pescado!*" they bawled. "*Pescado fresco!* Fish, fresh fish! Sardines, anchovy, squid, octopus! Fish at good prices!"

Their voices bounced off the walls, rattled the roof-tiles, put the sparrows to flight and echoed out across the sierras. Miles from the village you could hear their calls, scaring crows and rabbits and ricocheting through the olive groves. Only the sharp-tongued housewives seemed impervious as they haggled mercilessly over the price of a few sardines.

Late in the morning Paco appeared, crowned by a frayed trilby hat that looked even older than he. Stick in hand, he limped down the street behind his flock of goats. As their bells warned of their coming, neighbours' animals popped out of front doors to join the flock, which soon spread out over the surrounding hills.

The daily routine was one of the most reassuring features of village life. A weathered old man from the remote sierras would halt his mule and produce fresh, creamy goat cheeses from his baskets. The cries of an itinerant cobbler or the whitewash vendor offering newly-fired blocks of lime regularly echoed over the cobbles. Occasionally a plump gypsy woman with jet-black hair and golden earrings knocked at the door, selling flowers, shawls, or trinkets.

Pueblo life was fixed, immutable. Women sat crocheting in doorways while their husbands wove mats and baskets out of esparto grass. They tramped for miles into the sierras to harvest the esparto grass and to cut timber, for a miserable return; they ploughed with mules and cows, sowed and reaped by hand. Modern ways and amenities were penetrating, but slowly. Television had arrived, but the women still cooked on wood fires, and flush toilets and hot showers were little-known luxuries.

No man was alone with his girl until their wedding day, and after that he could expect to see her wearing black from head to foot for much of her life. For every relative that died, a woman was expected to go into mourning. It worked on a sliding scale. A cousin might merit a few weeks, an uncle two months, a mother several years. Usually a widow would shroud herself in black for the rest of her days. As the neighbours explained: "It's the custom." Remarrying was rare; it was not the custom.

From our terrace we looked down on a patchwork of ridiculously tiny fields. They were a triumph of human tenacity, created out of rocky infertile slopes by years of labour. First stone walls were built and then tons of earth carted in to construct the bancal, a terraced plot where sugar cane, sweet potatoes, beans and tomatoes flourished. Crop succeeded crop year-round for there was no real winter here at the southern edge of Europe. Irrigation channels traced glittering slivers of light between the fields, bringing water from the mountains as they had since Moorish times.

Beyond the fields, a thousand or so feet below us, lay the Mediterranean, shining like an ingot of beaten silver. Long ago, in the days of the Barbary pirates, raiders had come storming in to pillage the coast. That was one reason the *pueblo* was sited where it was, in a fortress-like position on top of a ridge. Perhaps it also explained why the inhabitants regarded the sea with suspicion and largely ignored it. They clung to the land and rarely ventured as far as the sea shore. Sometimes on the day of San Juan they might picnic there, but the most they would do is go for a paddle. No respectable woman, least of all a married one, could be seen in a bathing suit. That would change, but not for quite a few years yet.

Some days the sea appeared to fill the whole sky. Across this seamless backcloth, ships moved, but so slowly that they appeared motionless creations of an artist's brush. If you peered hard enough at the horizon at the right time of year, you could see the mountains of Africa. Or so everybody said, but I could never be sure whether I was looking at peaks or clouds. Nobody in the village had much curiosity about that land. It was the home of the *moros* and that was enough.

Behind the village there was no human habitation. Treeless mountains rose abruptly from dry riverbeds. If you penetrated the sierras, along overgrown tracks, you could surprise a wild goat or an eagle amid the crags and ravines. If you went far enough, you reached a pass from where you looked down on the province of Granada, a vista of pinewoods with trout streams running under their shade.

Once those mountain trails had been busy with mule-trains, carrying fish from the coast to Granada market, or loads of olive oil and flour, or contraband coffee. But new roads and motor transport had put paid to that. Even so, contact with the outside world was still limited. There were only five cars in a village of 2,000 people and few motor-cycles.

Strangers were still a novelty. Some villagers asked if I were a *francés*. Any non-Spaniard was thought to be French, probably because the last time foreigners had been seen in any numbers was in the Napoleonic Wars.

The 20th century had been a long time arriving in the *pueblo* and taking the bus to Málaga, the bustling provincial capital, was like stepping into a time machine. Many older villagers had never been

there and did not wish to go. The usual reason for making the journey was to visit a doctor and everybody knew what that meant. You ended up in hospital and came back in a coffin. Málaga was synonymous with death.

As for Madrid . . .

"*Hombre*, I did my military service in Madrid," said a neighbour. "I didn't like it. Their tomatoes were awful. Not a patch on the

15

ones we grow here."

Written down like that, it looks a clear enough statement. But spoken in the *pueblo's* individual style it was a different matter. The first time I heard excited *campesinos* discussing the potato crop, I could barely make out a word, despite the years I had struggled to master Castilian Spanish. The *pueblo* had its own dialect, with its own cadences and turns of phrase.

There is a musical lilt to the Andalusian accent that you don't find in severely correct Castilian. It is a language for poets, but in the mouths of the villagers it became something else again. Since few could decipher the written language, their knowledge was shaped by what they heard from the lips of parents and peers. Words took on strange forms as they happily dropped or inserted consonants, chewed up syllables, mispronounced letters. "*España*" became "*Epaña*", "*mucho*" became "*muncho*", "*bonito*" was "*boniko*", "*pescado*" was transformed into "*pecao*", "*moniato*" proved to be "*boniato*".

For all the charm of the *pueblo's* medieval life-style, there was a dark side to it. Physical and mental defects were common, some clearly due to in-breeding, others to neglect through ignorance and lack of facilities, for skilled attention could have remedied at least some of the bent limbs and minds. The *pueblo* had no dentist. Instead, a tooth-puller visited from time to time and grisly evidence of his work was everywhere.

Andalusia has spawned some of Spain's greatest poets, men like Alberti, Aleixandre, Cernuda, García Lorca, Góngora, the Machado brothers. A thousand years ago the caliph of Córdoba is said to have amassed a library of 400,000 books. Four hundred years ago Salamanca university's prestige attracted Europe's greatest thinkers. Unfortunately, all this erudition had done little for the *pueblo*. In fact, it had passed it right by; many of the older villagers could barely write their names, few of the younger ones ever glanced at a newspaper. When I unpacked half a dozen cheap paperbacks, Alcachofa, one of our poorest neighbours, so poor that the family could not even afford a radio, stared at them in wonder.

"Have you read all those?" she asked. "You must be very intelligent."

I could find nobody who played a musical instrument, not even the guitar, the quintessential instrument of Andalusia. The church had no organ, nor choir. There were no sports facilities, not even—in soccer-mad Spain —a stretch of ground flat enough for a football pitch, nor was there a team to play on it. Only a handful of families could afford to educate their children beyond primary school. Years of rigid, authoritarian rule had eroded enterprise and crushed initiative. Also there had been the bitter guerrilla war in this region after the Civil War, something about which we learned only through chance remarks. It was a subject the villagers preferred not to discuss, but I judged that much of the spirit had been hammered out of the village during those terrible years. The *pueblo* had endured, but at a cost.

It was just as well we were dedicated to the healthy simple life, for the latest medical facilities had yet to reach the *pueblo*, although it did have a doctor, it was unwise to fall sick. Disturbing stories circulated about what had happened to those who had been so careless as to do so. Emergency cases would be bundled into a taxi for the 90-minute journey over a winding, potholed road to the nearest hospital.

When I asked Alcachofa why the *pueblo* did not have an ambulance, she stared at me in perplexity.

"An ambulance? I never heard of such a thing. What's that?"

That the villagers lived as long as they did was a tribute to their resilience. Or their faith. When all else failed, the sick would sign on for a trip to "El Curandero", a healer who lived in the mountains of Granada and was said to effect amazing cures. I met him once. He was a young man with striking eyes and a certain charisma, but he was enigmatic about his curing methods. Patients arrived by the busload to seek his help and, although he had no set fees, they left behind enough thank-you gifts as well as their cast-off crutches to make Pepe El Santo a wealthy man.

3

THE STREET OF BITTERNESS

Although we lived at the top of the town, we were far removed from high society. Better-off villagers and the intellectual elite had larger houses on the main street. That was where you found the priest, the doctor, the miller, the bank manager, the coffin-maker and the school principal. Humbler folk lived in the Barrio Alto. That was okay. We were pretty humble ourselves and poorer than many of our neighbours despite their apparent lack of affluence.

Our street was called Calle Amargura, the Street of Bitterness. The name baffled me at first but later, toiling up the higgledy-piggledy cobbles, I understood how it could be likened to the Via Crucis, the Way of the Cross. At any rate it had a better ring to it than Railway Cuttings. The neighbours took a keen interest in the two visitors from Mars who had landed on their doorsteps. They knew precisely what furniture we had in our house because they watched us stagger up the street with every stick of it. We were treated to their opinions at every step, and then some more when they invited themselves in to inspect the premises.

"*Precioso*," they exclaimed, clearly staggered at our strange tastes, such as the revolutionary move of changing the ceiling colour from traditional yellow or green to boring old white. "*Precioso*," they muttered as they inspected our old tables and rush chairs, the sort of stuff they were throwing out to squeeze veneered cabinets and shiny plastic sofas into their tiny living rooms.

"*Y la tele?* And where is the television?" they asked.

We had no television and we did not want a telephone either. We had decided to live the simple life without such distractions. No wonder our neighbours, who had never had the privilege of rejecting such modern devices, gaped at us as though we were out of our minds.

"*Vaya con Dios. Adiós. Adiós,*" said the villagers as we passed. The little children, however, reacted differently when they sighted my bearded face.

"*Feo, feo.* Ugly, ugly," they cried, running inside or burying their faces in their mothers' skirts.

"Why don't you shave?" asked one young fellow. "Here nobody wears a beard—except queers."

It was a lot later, after Franco died, that facial hair became accepted as the badge of democrats.

Gardening was an ordeal at first. As I struggled to clear our small patch of weeds, I heard subdued comments and expressions of astonishment. Looking up, I discovered that every available rooftop appeared to be occupied by little women in black, watching my every move. Half the village was peering down on my vegetable patch. Every time I attempted to wrench some piece of vegetation from the earth, there would be a hissing noise and I would see heads shaking.

"No, not that one," they would advise, wagging their fingers negatively. I pointed to another plant and they smiled and nodded their heads. Out it came. The gallery debated, approved or rejected every move I made. Fortunately, after the first few sessions, they apparently decided I had passed my apprenticeship and left me in relative peace.

Fernando, lean as a whip with a Cockney chirpiness, took pity on me as I struggled in vain against slugs, snails, white-fly, leaf-curl, canker, blight, wilt, rust, rot, mites and mildew, all of which gave my garden a certain resemblance to the battlefield of the Somme. Chemical warfare was Fernando's solution. He had a poison for everything and, after dusting his own garden with enough venom to extinguish half the *pueblo*, he would hand me liberal doses of the deadly stuff.

When he worked as a gardener for wealthy foreigners down the valley, he often returned with strawberry, tomato or more exotic plants. "Gifts," he explained with a roguish smile, passing a few over. I followed his instructions carefully, secretly going easy on the insecticides, and watched my plants shrivel and die. His, within a few weeks, would be in glorious bloom.

Some things did grow, however. For the first time I could enjoy the inimitable lusciousness of sun-warmed peaches picked straight from the tree. Garlic flourished, defying the insect hordes, as long as it was planted in the right phase of the moon as recommended by Pura, my amiable octogenarian neighbour. Radishes shot up like weeds. Hibiscus and boungainvillea flourished and the sweet fragrance of Dama de Noche drenched the nights. Imported daffodils took time to acclimatise and then, under the impression that spring had arrived, sprang into bloom at Christmas.

One day I was smoothing flat a section of the garden when Pura came out to inspect the work. She had won Thea's heart from the first moment with her gift of a carnation and she soon became like a second mother. She passed on recipes, recalled local folklore, recommended herbal cures, and talked of events that stretched back to the last century. Although nearly 90, she was still spry in mind and body. She had experienced revolution and war and hunger, but retained a good-humoured resilience. For somebody who had rarely left the *pueblo*, she was amazingly open to new ideas. But my gardening activities bewildered her.

"What are you going to put there?" she inquired.

"A lawn." I told her.

"A lawn?" She was obviously baffled. "What's that?"

When I pointed to some blades of grass, she gaped.

"Weeds! But why on earth do you want to plant weeds?"

The question must have puzzled the whole street. They were equally puzzled by the fact that we did not employ anyone to dig our garden, nor to cook and clean. All *extranjeros* have big cars and lots of servants, don't they? And who ever heard of an *extranjero* whitewashing? How could a foreigner know the right technique?

They were right, of course. The first time I tried my hand at whitewashing, I climbed up to the terrace and began busily wielding a brush in the hope of sloshing on enough of the stuff to hold the house together for another few months. Although the uneven walls were nearly a metre thick, if you chipped a hole in one, the dust of centuries past flowed out. Frequent whitewashing was essential to keep it glued together.

Nothing could be more simple, I reflected, as I daubed the walls. The sun was pleasantly warm and only moderate amounts of burning lime splattered into my eyes. But yells of alarm from the street below soon told me something was seriously wrong. My brush was spraying a snowstorm over passing traffic. Alcachofa emerged on her terrace, inspected my work, and shook her head in disgust at my performance.

"No, not that way! Make shorter strokes. You've too much on the brush. You missed a bit over there. You've got it too thick..."

I tried to ignore these comments, but my morale was severely undermined. Then suddenly Alcachofa was by my side, grabbing the brush from my hand. She had crossed the street and swept straight through the house and up the stairs to rescue me from my foolishness.

"Look, this is the way to do it."

She may have been another Velázquez with the brush but, for a second or so, I was tempted to strangle her. Instead, I left her working away, went down to the living room and poured myself a brandy. By the time she came downstairs, breathing self-satisfaction at a good job well done, I was halfway through my book.

The menfolk reminded me frequently that they never took holidays; such luxuries were reserved for effete city-dwellers. Because they never saw me doing physical labour, they clearly imagined I was some sort of eccentric playboy who got his kicks from fiddling with a typewriter and a camera. It was difficult to persuade them that I was not a gentleman of leisure and indeed, as I saw them leading their mules out to the fields every day and plodding back at nightfall, their faces bruised by toil, their threadbare clothing stained with sweat, ambivalent feelings enveloped me. They were slaves of the soil, a fate from which only an accident of birth had saved me. By their standards, I *was* a playboy and I could not escape tremors of guilt.

Eventually the children became accustomed to my strange appearance and the witch-black old ladies no longer discussed in loud stage whispers our health and odd habits as we walked up the street. They even stopped offering us worm-eaten old furniture at outrageous prices, as the word got around that we were not really such a soft touch after all. In time, even El Chico hardly blinked at our passing. Even so, now and again he could not resist tugging at his chin, to indicate my beard, and spitting on the cobbles in disapproval.

El Chico lived just down the street and enjoyed the perfect life, for he simply had no inhibitions. He was the freest and most honest man in the *pueblo*, liberated from any need to conform to social convention. His mother dressed and fed him and he had nothing to do but amuse himself. When he sighted a mule going up the street, he hitched a free lift by clutching its tail. Whenever a band was playing, he would encourage the musicians with some inspired conducting. Any procession was fair game. He would join in, nodding and smiling—he had a particularly devilish smile—to bystanders. When a funeral cortege passed, he quickly took a leading place with the mourners, solemnly crossing himself and making signals to everybody to remove their hats.

Some said that El Chico was crazy. Others opined that he was the cleverest fellow in the village because, for El Chico, every day was a holiday. He had black beady eyes, a pronounced jaw and a tendency to utter strange noises rather than coherent speech, which alarmed the more sensitive strangers. But he was unfailingly good-tempered, and more than good-tempered when he sighted large-breasted females. El Chico indicated his pleasure with appropriate gestures and, occasionally, by exhibiting his considerable virility. Some women broke up in laughter. Others fled in terror.

But his favourite diversion was reserved for unsuspecting motorists. He stood by the roadside, posing as a hitchhiker. Innocently, a stranger would halt and El Chico, grinning broadly, would jump in, pointing down the road. When they reached the next town, the motorist waited for his passenger to descend, but El Chico made no move. Instead, he pointed back up the hill. Thinking that there had been a misunderstanding, the obliging motorist would drive back to the village. Once there, El Chico again made no move to alight. Grinning ever more diabolically, he pointed back down the hill. El Chico did not have such a bad life.

The day we discovered that we had acquired an *apodo*, nickname, it seemed that we were truly on the way to some degree of acceptance in the community. The *pueblo*-dwellers as a whole were known as *los aguanosos* (the watery ones). There were two theories about how this came about, either because we had abundant supplies of water or because the village had once been renowned for the juicy apricots it produced.

In addition, every family had a nickname, by which its members were usually identified. Ask where you could find Eusebio Dominguez and you would get nowhere. Use his *apodo* and there would be no problem. Everybody knew who were *Malavista, El Canario, El Zorro, El Pincho, Pichica, Picamanos, El Rubio, El Moreno, El Colorín...* It was advisable to tread carefully when using these names as some were clearly abusive and you might be talking to one of the same family, so inter-related were the villagers.

Our *apodo* was inherited from the family who had sold us the house and, although the origins of many nicknames had been lost in the mists of time, ours came with an unusual explanation. It was born in an era when the local *cacique* (overlord) used to ride about the fields urging his workers to greater efforts for their five or six pesetas a day. A young member of the family, eager to better himself, went hat in hand to this landowner to plead for financial help for his education. He wanted to get on in the world (*hacer carrera*), he explained. "So you want a career? Then why don't you make one to the next town?" scoffed the great man, playing on the double meaning of *carrera* (career and race or run). The contemptuous jibe entered into local folklore. Henceforth, the family was known as *La Carrería*, and we in turn became *Los de la Carrería*.

Bizarre though our ideas were, incomprehensible though some of our actions must have appeared, the *pueblo* accepted our presence and little by little influenced our ways. The longer we lived in the village, the more we unconsciously tended to adopt village attitudes. Soon, when strangers came wandering through, I found myself pausing to scrutinise them with the same curiosity as the locals. Who were they? What were they doing here?

It became difficult to drag oneself away from the intimate, protective atmosphere of the village. The outside world was strange and threatening compared to our sheltered life on the Street of Bitterness. The *pueblo* enfolded us, as safe and comforting as the womb.

4

SPRING RITES

Dive-bombers signalled that spring had arrived. They came in the form of swifts. Formations of them appeared abruptly one morning, wheeling above the rooftops, emitting piercing cries. Celebrating their return from winter quarters in Africa, they skimmed chimney-pots, terraces and television aerials with dizzy abandon, flying straight at walls and windows, only avoiding collision at the last, breath-taking moment. They did it just for the hell of it, just because they were glad to be back.

They were a sure indicator that winter was over, one of those rituals that marked the seasons in the *pueblo* as surely as any calendar dates or changing temperatures. It was the way it had always been. Everything had its allotted place, everybody knew the part he or she had to play.

One particularly brilliant spring morning, when we walked into the hills, stands out in the memory. We were on our way to a picnic at Antonio and Caridad's farm.

"Come and feast on baby goat," Antonio had said. "It will be a great day."

Paquito danced ahead, chasing birds and butterflies. His sisters ran to pick the flowers blooming yellow, white and lilac along the way. Thrushes and finches squabbled amid the olive groves and almond trees. The sun warmed our backs as we tramped up a narrow track, beaten down by generations of men and their beasts of burden. It wound past tumbledown farmhouses and ranks of neatly-pruned vines. Here and there a mule dozed in the shade, flicking its ears at the buzzing flies.

Men working the land cried greetings as we passed.

"*Vaya con Dios!* Go with God!"

One insisted we halt and enter his *cortijo*. It was whitewashed and cool inside. There were two rush chairs and a rickety table on a floor of rough concrete. A hoe leaned against the wall next to several large wine barrels. The farmer picked up a bamboo rod with a cup chipped out at the end, dipped it into a barrel and filled hastily-cleaned glasses with amber liquid. He waited expectantly for our praise as we gulped the strong, sweet Moscatel wine.

There were no roads where we walked. The only sounds to break the stillness were the murmur of insects, the slice of an axe, or the cries of a ploughman urging on his animals. Orchids, irises, lavender, rosemary and thyme spread their colour and aroma over track and hillside. A host of butterflies swirled up at our passing, a fluttering, flirting rainbow of Clouded Yellows, Painted Ladies, and Swallowtails that easily dodged Paquito's pursuing hands.

Innocence shone from Paquito's eyes, as dark as treacle and as deep as a pit. At four, he knew nothing and everything. He was already a true *macho*, indulged outrageously by his mother.

"*Qué malo! Qué malo eres, luz de mi vida!* How bad you are, light of my life!" she would cry approvingly, when he tortured his sisters or pulled the cat's tail.

At the farm, Antonio hauled a bleating baby goat on to the patio.

"The truth is I never like doing this," he said, before he matter-of-factly sacrificed it for our lunch. The goat was skinned, cleaned, and cut into chunks, which were tossed into a pan bubbling with olive oil, saffron, onions, garlic and tomatoes. We ate platefuls of stewed kid and breathed garlic all over one another and sank glass after glass of sweet Moscatel wine, then we dozed in the heat and listened to the cicadas and dreamed that the afternoon would never end.

On the homeward journey, when the village came into view, it was a rosy mirage against the dark mountains, the house windows transformed into diamonds by the rays of the lowering sun.

Paquito gave up chasing butterflies and turned those dark eyes on me with the childlike trust that instantly makes you feel old.

"Aveed!" he said, doing the best he could with my name.

"*Sí, Paquito?*"

"Aveed, are there butterflies in your *pueblo?*"

One of the rites of spring was with the sugar-cane harvest along the coast. It was an opportunity for fit young men to earn extra money, although the wages were miserable enough and the work was dirty and exhausting. It was also a chance to escape the *pueblo's* iron rules of conduct for a while. There were unattached girls down on the coast and American bars and *salas de fiestas* and the *pueblo* gossips were far away. Since the 19th century, the powerful Larios family had owned large stretches of coastal lowland and the farmers, in semi-feudal fashion, had been obliged to supply their sugar mills. But sugar cane was a dying industry. It was proving more profitable to plant apartment blocks in the cane fields and the mills were closing.

Early potatoes, the big spring crop around the *pueblo*, were losing out too. Prices went up and down without rhyme or reason. Every year it was a gamble and often the farmers were lucky to break even after months of labour.

"It's the middlemen," pronounced my neighbour Miguel. "They fix the prices and we just accept them like idiots, then they resell at big profits in the markets. We should all get together and market the potatoes ourselves, but trying to organise people here is like fighting your way through quicksand."

Out beyond the Rio Seco, a Dutchman was said to be experimenting with new crops, with fruit bushes from America, but everybody knew foreigners had crazy ideas. And what could a

Dutchman know of sub-tropical conditions? The farmers stuck obstinately to what they knew, potatoes, tomatoes, sweet potatoes, beans, and more potatoes. It was some years before the potato plots began giving way to fields of bushy, fleshy-leafed trees. Few had heard of an avocado when we first came to the *pueblo*. Then word spread of vast profits and avocadoes became the rage. Vines were ripped up, new terraces carved out and irrigated. The new wonder tree was planted everywhere, but had anybody researched the market? Would there still be sufficient demand in five or 10 years' time?

Meanwhile, the old rituals went on. Everybody had a part to play in *Semana Santa*, a piece of religious theatre with hints of the pagan past. It began two days before Palm Sunday with the procession of *María Santísima de los Dolores* and reached a climax at midnight on Good Friday. The *hermandades* (brotherhoods or clubs) prepared all year for these processions, each trying to outdo the other and put on a good show, raising cash to buy finery encrusted with silver and gold and precious stones for the Virgin, to gild her throne or improve the lighting. Pride and prestige were involved and the position of *hermano mayor* (the chief brother) was highly coveted. Later, changing times and greater prosperity sparked the creation of a new brotherhood. It was dubbed the *Hermandad* of the Yuppies by more cynical villagers, for it was clearly more opulent than its rivals and its members cut splendid figures as they paced through the village in dazzling silky tunics and cloaks.

On the nights of the processions, the *pueblo* vibrated with excitement. Anonymous, robed figures strode about the streets, greeting friends and relatives. These *hermanos* had a sinister aspect, until they flipped back the hoods covering their faces to reveal earthy, rubicund, familiar features. They filled the bars with noise and laughter, ordering beer and wine, joking and arguing. To an impressionable visitor it was like straying into a Ku Klux Klan social club.

"*Oiga!*" somebody keeping watch at the door would call. "Here comes the priest! Time to go."

Hurriedly, they would finish their tapas and drinks, flip the hoods over their faces and disappear into the night. A dozen wore no hoods but donned painted masks representing the 12 Apostles, while others played the part of Roman centurions. Nobody was in the least selfconscious about his annual public performance or indeed thought twice about it. These were roles they were proud to play, handed down through the generations.

My neighbour Miguel, who never struck me as particularly devout, took part in the processions. I watched him dress for the occasion, donning the black tunic of a penitent, tightening a cord around his waist, arranging the scapula and covering his face with a black hood. He peered out from two eyeholes. It was no longer Miguel. It was somebody else. But he still spoke with Miguel's voice.

"When I was really sick," he told me. "I vowed that if I recovered I would walk in the procession of the *Virgen* and *Jesús el Nazareno* for three years in thanks for my deliverance. And so I shall. It's a small price to pay for what was close to a miracle."

What the villagers agreed on was that a real miracle took place during the highlight of the week, the women's procession.

"Imagine it," they said. "All the women of the *pueblo* take part and they must not chat to one another the whole time. Now that is asking something!"

Young and old, dressed from top to toe in black, the women filed from the church at midnight on Good Friday. The lights of the *pueblo* were extinguished and the only illumination came from the candles carried by the women. They walked silently up the stepped streets in two files as the rest of the village looked on from windows, doorways and balconies. There was the scuffle of feet on cobbles, the rustle of skirts, a low murmur of voices (it was asking for a miracle), and—far at the rear—the thump of staves on stone as the bearers of the Virgin began their march. A hush of expectancy hung over the darkened *pueblo* in the sierra night.

Then, in unison, in clear firm voices that raised the hairs on one's neck and sent prickles up and down the spine of believers and unbelievers alike, they started to sing.

Sálvame, Virgen María,

Oyeme te imploro con fé,

Mi corazón en ti confía,

Virgen María, sálvame.

(Save me, Virgin Mary,

Hear me, I implore you with faith,

My heart trusts in you,

Virgin Mary, save me.)

The women's voices flowed and ebbbed as they climbed to the Barrio Alto and paced the twisting streets, singing to the Virgin and joining her in her grieving. The flickering candlelight softened the outlines of the strong, deep-etched features of the old and leant mystery to the smooth, ingenuous faces of the young. Six men had the honour of carrying the Virgin, her frozen grief and resplendent gown dazzlingly lit by battery-powered bulbs. They paused to rest frequently,

then at a signal would shoulder their burden again, swaying her around the bends, carefully dodging street-lamps and balconies, treading gingerly over the uneven cobbles as they began the steep descent of the Street of Bitterness

The women's voices surged and faded, echoing and re-echoing, gradually dying away as the procession negotiated the narrow streets and slowly returned to the church plaza. Next morning, the hot wax from their candles lay congealed on the cobbles, a prosaic reminder of the deep emotions stirred the night before.

The Day of the Cross, May 3, was a very different affair. By May the days were already balmy and the countryside was a riot of wild flowers. Spring fever gripped the *pueblo* and made this day, full of pagan references, the most light-hearted of the year. Carnations, lilies and all manner of greenery were woven into crosses set up around the village, each street, each corner competing with the others to put on a better show. Canopies kept off the sun, the walls were hung with old artefacts from esparto sandals to oil lamps, and tables were loaded with wine, sausage, olives and ham. Strangers or neighbours, whoever came wandering by to admire and comment on the crosses and the general decoration, would be invited to eat and drink.

A group of youngsters paraded through the village with guitar and accordion, singing love songs to giggling girls. They were the *Mayeros*, reviving a tradition that disappeared when the Civil War devastated the country in the 1930s. For three days, from midnight to dawn, the *Mayeros* would go from house to house, serenading the young girls, praising their beauty and telling them the names of their admirers. On the Day of the Cross, if a *maya* had shown interest in one of her suitors, he would offer her a present.

"*Hombre!* In those days meeting a girl wasn't easy," explained Manolo el Panadero, a retired baker who was something of a walking history book and a famed *Mayero*. "Why, if a girl met her novio (fiancé) in the street, she would dash into the nearest house out of embarrassment. It just wasn't done for a couple to meet and talk as they do now. And as for kissing!

"I used to sing a song to each girl naming those who asked for her hand. She would be inside, maybe pretending not to hear, but she was listening all right. In fact, all the girls would be listening to see how many suitors each had. I tell you, many a couple has me to thank for getting them together."

Manolo was the last of a breed. His vast repertoire of songs and rhyming couplets, some hilarious, others scurrilous, about the village and its people formed an oral history in a community where few had ever known how to read and write. And he sang superbly. At Easter, the processions would halt by an appropriate balcony for Manolo to launch a *saeta*, a *flamenco* "arrow" of adoration for the *Virgen* or of lamentation for the death of Christ.

The *Mayos* were songs of a different stripe, full of amorous imagery: "You are a beautiful garden/You are a delicate flower/If you accept me as your *novio*/Come out on your balcony." If you were looking for a real over-the-top *piropo* to win the heart of a woman, Manolo could oblige with such verses as "All the flowers were born/on the same day as you/ and in the baptismal font/ the nightingales sang too (*El día que tu naciste/nacieron todas las flores,/ y en la pila del bautismo/ cantaron los ruiseñores*)."

Manolo thought—and I had to agree with him—that there was a good deal more romance in those innocent lines than in the stuff they were dishing out at the *pueblo*'s latest symbol of progress, a disco.

5

TO HAVE AND TO HOLD

Spring meant a new life for Alberto. It brought him happy release from his sharp-tongued sister-in-law, cheerless father-in-law, taciturn brother and a chorus of bawling children, with whom he shared three rooms. And it meant he could go to live in a palace, even if it was next door and he had to build it himself.

Alberto was getting married. This was quite an achievement since he was far from being the arrogant Latin lover. Rather, he was a little reserved, a definite handicap in a village where bachelors far outnumbered available girls. But he was presentable and amiable and, in the magic way that these things happen, he snagged Conchita, a girl from a distant village, who shared her home with parents and grandparents and innumerable brothers and sisters. It was quite an achievement for her, too. Alberto drew out his life savings and prepared to enshrine her in a style neither he nor she had ever been accustomed to.

In the past, newly-weds had often squeezed in with in-laws, but increasing affluence brought new trends. These days they expected to start married life in imitation-celebrity style copied from gossip magazine picture spreads, where starlets and playboys displayed their glittery tastes. Friends and relatives were invited to tour the new quarters, so that they could properly admire the gleaming suites of veneered furniture, the washing machine, and the outsize television. A lifetime of sweat and callouses had usually gone into creating these gilded cages, stuffed with enough napery, drapery and cutlery to stock a Holiday Inn.

Alberto was not going to be outdone and he worked from dawn to dusk aiding the builders. After months of labour, the house was finally finished, the latest consumer goods were manhandled up the street to the admiration and wonderment of the neighbours, and the wedding day was fixed.

Alberto's old home did not have a kitchen or bathroom, unless you counted the washbasin in a corner of the stable. His new one had everything. No wonder he glowed with pride as he showed visitors around. Opulent-looking marble had been used on the front steps and the staircase and polished to slippery death-trap perfection. One wall of the parlour was covered by a huge cabinet, in glossy veneer with anodised fittings. Gilded pottery cherubs and a plaster cast of an astonishingly erotic nude negress were arrayed along the shelves. Alberto snapped open drawers to reveal embroidered table-cloths and gleaming cutlery.

An outsize television dominated the tiny living room where Alberto and his family would spend their evenings, for the parlour was strictly for show. A refrigerator and a washing machine—a washing machine in the *Barrio Alto*!—had been squeezed into the miniature kitchen. No debt had been spared in creating this wonderland.

"Look at this!" said Alberto, nonchalantly indicating a plastic coat-rack cunningly moulded into the shape of deer antlers.

"I bought that in Germany when I was a guest worker. Oh, do you want to smoke?"

He picked up a plastic donkey from the table, something about his manner indicating that this was the *pièce de resistance*. He held out the donkey and then, delighted at my puzzlement, laughed.

"Here, take a cigarette."

He raised the donkey's tail and out of its anal cavity popped a cigarette.

"Clever, eh? From Germany, you know."

Village weddings had a flavour all their own. They were not quiet decorous affairs. They were not private either. Only a boorish, parsimonious type would have tried to keep the big day to himself and family. The whole *pueblo* invited itself. However hard the families involved had to labour to scrape together the cash, the floodgates opened on a wedding day and the pesetas flowed like coñac. Thus, a bus was hired to transport guests to the ceremony in Conchita's village.

Among the bus passengers was an impeccably turned-out young man, hair smoothed, shirt spotless, suit pressed until the creases could have sliced *pepinos*. It was some moments before I recognised Alberto. I had always thought a hoe grew out of his right arm. Away from his usual environment, he seemed a different person. The other male guests had not gone quite so far. Leathery, sunburnt throats burst from open-necked shirts and they rested their large, work-hardened hands carefully on their best pants. Their wives, wobbling in incredibly high heels, were resplendent in glossy synthetic prints.

After the intimacy of the *pueblo*, the outside world seemed a strange, hostile place and the village folk reacted by drawing into themselves a little. They bolstered their courage and confidence during the journey by swapping obscene jokes about the bizarre habits of those who did not have the good fortune to be part of our community. The bus lurched around curve after curve for about an hour before depositing us at our destination. The bride's village proved to be smaller than our *pueblo* and comparatively poverty-stricken. The wedding was the biggest thing that had happened in years and we visitors from another planet were the focus of attention.

Everybody was out on their doorsteps to inspect us and to await a glimpse of the bride, who was preparing for the great moment in the family home. This primitive dwelling would have fitted into a corner of the palatial new residence awaiting her. Half the local population seemed to be crammed inside, exchanging gossip, offering advice, discussing the bride's dress. Since everybody was talking at the tops of their voices, nobody could hear a word. But it did not matter. Everybody was having a good time. Except maybe the bride herself, who was in the usual state of shock. Alberto was smiling a lot but found it difficult to speak.

Wandering around the village, we inspected the quality of the whitewashing, the general state of repair, the crops growing in nearby fields. Compared to our *pueblo*, we agreed, it wasn't up to much. The local wine was tested, too. It was made from identical grapes and in exactly the same way as the wine in our *pueblo*, but it was clear to us all—it just did not measure up. Fortunately, before conversation turned to the next obvious topic, the relative qualities of the two villages' women, the bride appeared, dazzling in her long white gown. Arm in arm with her fiancé's brother, she set off around the village, dodging stray goats and the traces of passing mules, followed by the groom escorting her sister, dozens of relatives, neighbours and whoever cared to join in. The procession wound around the tiny *pueblo* several times and, just as everyone was becoming a little dizzy, entered the church.

They don't often have weddings in that village and nobody wanted to miss the free entertainment. The church was wall to wall with people. Children giggled and ran up the aisles and a couple of mongrel dogs sniffed about the pews. The congregation was as well behaved as usual. The priest only had to raise his voice a little above the general hum of conversation. After the formalities he lectured the couple severely on their future responsibilities.

Only one guest had a camera, which refused to work after the second shot so we were spared the spectacle I had encountered at my previous village wedding. Professionals had been called in for that one and throughout the ceremony they thrust cameras in the priest's and couple's faces and let off flashes. This torture was accepted without a murmur as part of the ritual. The reception had been equally memorable. It had been held in a draughty, concrete-floored barn, outside which the guests waited for an hour or so while the bride and groom were away being photographed in every conceivable pose—a shot of them gazing into each other's eyes while sitting on the matrimonial bed was a feature of many wedding albums. Only when the barn doors were finally unlocked had I appreciated the need for rigid security. Parents and children fell on the drink and refreshment with an amazing voracity. The wedding cake, whose fifteenth tier just brushed the ceiling, was toppled and disappeared to the last crumb.

Alberto's reception proved to be a little different. For one thing, the affair was not held in anything so down-market as a barn or garage. After outbursts of coughing and a choir of bawling children had silenced the priest and avalanches of rice had been hurled on the church steps, reducing the bride to a pulp, we swept off to one of the *pueblo*'s two bars.

Whether or not Alberto and his bride were actually there, I shall never know. It was impossible to see. It was impossible to breathe, too. There was no Matterhorn of a wedding cake. Or, if there was one, the crush was so great that I never even glimpsed it. A dozen local children gazed with hungry, wondering eyes through the barred window as snacks of cured ham and sausage arrived and vanished in 20 seconds. Everybody drank Cuba Libre, a name for rum and cola coined after the Cuban Revolution. In the *pueblo*, Cuba Libre meant any mix of drinks, from whisky and tonic to vodka and orange, though gin and cola was the favourite mix. Dispensing with glasses, each armed with a bottle of Pepsi and a bottle of gin, my fellow guests dropped all decorum and unleashed themselves in a short-lived bacchanal. There was little con-versation in the tight-packed bar, as the food was finished off and the bottles passed swiftly from hand to hand. The watching kids had infil-trated and I watched fascinated as 40 per cent proof gurgled down the throat of an eight-year-old.

Suddenly, after 30 minutes, it was over. The booze had run out. Everyone was smiling, however, including an aging neighbour who, in all the time I had known him, had never permitted so much as a flicker of humour or any other known emotion to traverse his worn features. Every day I had wished him "Buenos días" without a word of reply escaping his lips. I had tried to discuss the weather with him, the potato harvest, the state of the stock market. Nothing. He had remained mute, a shrunken, distant figure sitting on his doorstep as though part of the stonework.

One night everybody had run on to their terraces to gaze at a forest fire raging over a ridge near the village. It was so close that it seemed the flames jumping from pine to pine might engulf the houses. The air was heavy with the smell of burning resin and drifting ash. During this dramatic incident, I had glanced down into the street and there was my neighbour, as imperturbable as ever, sitting on his doorstep as usual. He continued to stare straight ahead at the wall opposite, without any indication of alarm or interest, totally ignoring the shooting flames.

Yet now he was not just smiling. He was beaming. His eyes were shining and he looked at me as though seeing me for the first time. And he spoke.

"You like Spain?"

"*Sí, señor!*"

He smiled and nodded. The ice had been broken. After that he acknowledged my existence and quite frequently we exchanged greet-ings. Our conversation never advanced any further, however. Which was just as well, for I don't know what I would have replied had he asked me what I thought of weddings.

6

THE GRAPEVINE

"*Daveed! Daveed! Teléfono!*"

I sprang from my chair and made for the door. Dolores was outside, beckoning anxiously and pointing to her shop up the street. I sprinted over the cobbles and up the steps, elbowed aside an old lady who was feeling the tomatoes, sent oranges and potatoes rolling over the floor, gasped for breath and grabbed the receiver. There was a click at the other end. Too late, again.

For quite a while, even though it was just around the corner from our house, I had not been aware of the existence of Dolores's grocery shop, for there was no sign outside. Later, when she installed a public telephone, I got to know it pretty well. Many an hour I sat among the salted sardines and the detergents waiting to call while listening to a neighbour indulging in baby talk with one of her grandchildren at the other end of the village. Anybody can ask for a reverse charge call, but try it when Alcachofa is prodding you aside to reach the haricot beans. Extracting information from a government department is never an easy task, but imagine the difficulties when Dolores is slicing ham inches away from your right ear.

"What's that strange noise? Is somebody dying?" callers would ask. How could I explain to them that it was only Manolo the fisherman advertising his wares?

But Dolores's telephone was an improvement on previous arrangements when the nearest receiver had been in a corner of the Casino bar. Only Antonio, the avuncular proprietor, knew how to operate that museum piece.

I tried to dial numbers time and again without success, until Antonio took pity on me and dialled them himself. A safecracker's skill was required, as he demonstrated, dialling slowly with precisely-timed pauses. Finally, I would get through, but it was hardly worth the effort. Fuzzy voices from a long way away shouted unmentionable things down a line that seemed to be under water. Although I had a finger plugged into my free ear, it could not block out the bar noises, the television, the braying of a donkey tethered in the street.

"So call me back in half an hour when you have the information," an optimistic friend at the other end of the line might say. He would ring off and that was the last time we ever made contact.

It was the march of progress that was the problem. The telephone had gone automatic. When we first arrived in the *pueblo*, things had been better. You went to Ima's house and told her the number you wanted. Then you went for a stroll, had a coffee and a chat. By the time you came back, Ima had performed some magic with the plugs and you were through.

My hours in Antonio's bar and among Dolores's vegetables convinced me that I needed a telephone, but years went by without the men from the Telefónica company connecting me. In those days none of my neighbours had a telephone or saw any need for one. Few of them could afford a radio and the television sets, black and white, were largely confined to the bars. When somebody bought a set, for status reasons they ordered the largest screen available. Then they installed it in a room two metres by two metres, which made for uncomfortable viewing and serious eye-strain.

Fortunately, the art of conversation did not lapse. The *pueblo* women may have distrusted telephones but they were expert communicators. They knew most things before they happened. As for events outside the *pueblo*, these made little or no impact. Only a few copies of the local daily newspaper, *Sur de Málaga*, arrived on the morning bus, one to be delivered to the town hall, one for the bar. In any case, it contained precious little genuine news. It was a museum piece, full

of flowery language and calls for long life for El Caudillo, Generalísimo Franco. Events had to pass through the government propaganda filter. The image presented was of a world in turmoil, beset by Communist conspiracies, violent crime, natural disasters and Machiavellian politicians. What a contrast was Spain, if you were to believe the regime's tightly controlled media! Here, under the protection of a benign patriarch, all was tranquillity, prosperity and contentment.

When he learned I was a journalist, one villager scratched his head. "You write for newspapers? Nobody reads them here. We don't need them. We know everything that goes on."

And so they did. Nothing could work more efficiently than the village grapevine. One day I visited a village several hours' walk away and knocked on the door of an acquaintance. There was no response so I walked home. No road ran between the two villages, no vehicle traffic passed between the two, but my neighbour's first question—and she did not have a telephone—was "So did you find Don Felipe in the end?"

To maintain their secrets, adulterers must have been either very ingenious or phenomenally fast working, for every doorway and window had its vigilante in widow's weeds. Any hanky-panky would have been general knowledge before the sinner's feet hit the floor.

The neighbours' concern for our welfare was both comforting and suffocating. We had no need to lock a door for anybody entering our house would be seen by a dozen neighbours. By the same token, when by chance a male friend knocked on our door the day after I had left for a trip, the gossip mills went into over-drive.

Since the main purpose of going to the village shop was to keep up with the local news, the cramped space was always full of housewives who had just dropped in to buy one egg and two beans. Shopping for food could take a whole morning. It could be hazardous, too. Sometimes Thea would trip off to buy a few vegetables and weave back in a happy alcoholic cloud. That was the danger if one stopped to buy produce laid out in villagers' front parlours. Every house had its 500-litre barrel of Moscatel wine and there was considerable pressure for visitors to help empty it.

The gossipers were never short of a subject as long as Caridad was around. Unlike the other married women in the street, Caridad had preserved her figure. She was quick of wit, flashing of eye, and protected her three young children like a tigress. But she was an outcast. She did not come from the village and she was too spirited to meekly accept local ways. She also was possessed of a fearsome temper and a fiery tongue. When Caridad unleashed a string of expletives, the street quaked. So did Manolo the fish vendor. When he weighed out some sardines for Caridad, she would quickly double-check it on her own scales, using a kilo of potatoes as she had no weights. Caridad could not read or write, but she had an abacus lodged in her brain. Let the price be a peseta out and she would reduce Manolo to chopped *pulpo*.

Shortly after purchasing our house, we had to leave for several months and I entrusted the key to Caridad. When I came back, it was clear that for once the grapevine had not functioned and I was not expected. I detected an air of surprise and anticipation as I walked up the street, and soon found out why. A baby's cot sat in our living room. Wondering what it was doing there, I glanced out of the window and saw a goat browsing about the garden. As I watched, a neighbour appeared and quickly hauled it off down the street.

Caridad put on a brave front when I inquired about the cot. There had been an emergency, she explained casually, and a baby had slept the night there. Later, her children inadvertently spilled the beans. A family had lived rent-free in our house for some time, thanks to Caridad's generous loan of the key.

"What do you expect?" asked Alcachofa. "That Caridad is bad news."

Caridad's physical attractiveness did not endear her to the neighbours. Mothers were supposed to be plump and placid, not sexy firebrands. Fatness was equated with beauty and contentment and, a hangover from the lean years of the past, with prosperity. What sort of a husband was it who could not keep his wife well fed?

"Ay, how new you look!" would chant the neighbours in praise of a friend whose bulging flesh had ironed out the wrinkles in her face. Caridad's lack of kilos was a constant affront so, in a desperate attempt to become more acceptable, she went on a diet. She tossed back dozens of pills and ate mountains of bread and fried food. Soon she developed the beginnings of a double chin, her waist thickened and her health went into decline, but her popularity did not increase. She was "putting the horns in," murmured the gossips, meaning that she was two-timing her husband. Caridad could not win.

As long as you did not come into open conflict with local mores, however, in times of need the neighbours would be there to help. News of calamities spread with amazing rapidity and sometimes the show of solidarity was overwhelming. When a neighbour broke her leg, within half an hour I counted 15 people crowded into her living room and another 20 in the street discussing details of the case.

Death brought the whole village together. The first indication of a sad event was the daunting sight of phalanxes of sturdy matrons advancing arm-in-arm along the street, converging on the house of the deceased. Relations and friends began arriving from all points of the compass to offer their condolences in the traditional way. Afterwards, the men would emerge and stand in groups outside the house, smoking heavily and talking in muted tones. The women sat inside, sharing the family grief with often noisy lamentations.

All night and the following day the vigil continued, until the funeral in the evening when six men would hoist the coffin to their shoulders and carry it through the *pueblo* up the hill to the cemetery, followed by all the menfolk. You knew a cortege was approaching when you heard the murmur of many animated voices along the main street, for though a funeral had its solemn moments nobody was inhibited from taking advantage of the occasion. It was a chance for friends and family to meet and exchange the latest news.

Often, when the moment came to slide the coffin into a niche in the cemetery wall, there would be a slight hiccup: it would not fit. Then, as the relatives stood by, Manolo the cemetery keeper would climb up on the scaffolding, strip all decoration from the coffin and chip away at the niche until finally the box could be inserted. Finally, he would mix his cement, whack down some bricks and wall up the departed. On one occasion, when all his efforts to ram home a coffin were in vain, he disappeared for 10 minutes while mourners exchanged bewildered looks. Then he returned and muttered: "Ok, bring it over here. I've found another spot." And the coffin was shouldered again and whisked around the corner. Sometimes there was a further delay while Manolo opened the coffin and dumped inside it a large plastic bag containing the dessicated remains of relatives who had earlier occupied the family niche.

Although to an outsider these goings-on appeared upsetting and macabre, to say the least, the villagers took it in their stride. Such things happened at funerals. Nobody questioned the rituals handed down over generations. Even so, there were occasional surprises. Thus, when an 80-year-old neighbour lost one of her sons, the wake took the usual course. For 24 hours there was coming and going and the grieving mother sat pallid and exhausted in her living room receiving commiserations until the appointed hour.

But this time there was no burial. The actual funeral was taking place in Argentina, where the son had migrated 30 years earlier. The village grapevine, and village solidarity, spanned oceans.

7

WHEN THE LIVING IS EASY

Summer really began with the crack of a rocket in early June. It announced the start of the feria, our annual fair, when the *pueblo* downed tools for a week and everybody worked strenuously at letting their hair down. José was in charge of the rockets and he took the task seriously. Garbed in near-spotless bright blue dungarees, he held the rocket in one hand and then applied a lighted cigarette to the fuse. He would chat nonchalantly away as the fuse sputtered, then at precisely the right moment—a split second before it would be necessary to call a doctor and send out a search party for his arm—he released the rocket and it soared into the clear morning air above the *pueblo* to explode with a satisfying bang.

It awakened us at about 8am. Then there came an equally familiar sound from the far side of the village, as of an animal in pain, the strident, unmistakable notes of a band gearing up for an orgy of marches and *paso dobles*. Clarinet, trombones and trumpets burst into clamorous action, the drums thudded and the band was on its way through the echoing streets. It could not be ignored, especially as the players' efforts were punctuated by more suicidal rocket launching by José.

Finally, the band turned a corner and passed right beneath our window, bravely punching out Y Viva España. On the first occasion we gazed down from our terrace, we could not believe our eyes or ears. The band was composed of a mixture of 10-year-olds and pensioners, wearing whatever clothes had come to hand that morning. Village bands are notoriously out of tune, but this one pushed discordance to new levels. As it turned out, this was not our band. The *pueblo* did not have one, so the musicians had been imported at vast expense from a neighbouring village.

"Why are we paying good money for this? We could do better ourselves," said one or two more dynamic villagers and went to work to create a proper band. A music teacher was recruited and soon he was rehearsing 50 local schoolchildren until they had blisters in places they did not know existed. Diabolical sounds emerged as day and night they tootled away. But, at the band's first public appearance arrayed in resplendent blue uniforms, it was an instant success. It was no contest, really. Unlike the minstrels who had previously paraded our streets, they did not need heavy doses of brandy and *anís* to inspire them. Not only was it possible to recognise what they were playing but actually to enjoy listening to it.

Soon every mother wanted to have her child in the band and all the other villages competed to hire it for their *fiestas*. But our *feria* came first. Officially this annual binge did not start until the saint's day but, from the moment the first trailer came lumbering up the valley and began disgorging dodgem cars, the village was "in *fiesta*." It was impossible to plan any major work for weeks beforehand. A plumber or a builder would scratch his head, look doubtful, then say: " After the *feria*, okay?"

On San Antonio's day, the band pumped up the atmosphere with a tour of the village and a serenade in the church plaza. Young men in Córdoba hats, tight jackets and leather leggings paraded their carefully-groomed horses and mules up and down, pretending to ignore the groups of girls who giggled together in their vivid *gitano* dresses. Tight around the bosom, exploding in frills below the waist, those dresses made even the plainest girls look glamorous, as they fluttered their fans, tossed their hair, flounced and swirled about the *plaza*. Ay, the girls of the *pueblo*! Wicked-eyed, with cheeks like peaches and tongues like knives.

José set off a crescendo of rockets and the band struck up triumphantly as the saint's carved image was borne from the church and

placed in a cart decked with palm leaves, red and white carnations and bunting. The *romería* (pilgrimage) was under way. The pilgrims were known as *romeros* because rosemary (romero) was their symbol and they tucked the herb in hats or hair. The mounted contingent stepped haughtily through the main street, girls side-saddle behind the boys, while decorated carts followed, packed with children. Then came San Antonio, jolting along impassively in his cart, hauled by two cows that had been given the day off from ploughing. Behind came the villagers on foot and a posse of teenagers emitting *macho* mating calls on their silencer-free motor-cycles.

The cavalcade slowly wended its way down to the river-bed, past pink-blooming oleander bushes, and along to a pine-shaded spot where you could dip your feet in clear water gushing down from the sierra and listen to the cicadas. There, an animated, gargantuan picnic was held. The *romeros* consumed a few hundred kilos of barbecued meat, helped along with large quantities of beer and soft drinks. When they were near to bursting, the menfolk leaned back on the pine needles and dozed while the women gossiped behind their fans. From time to time somebody would break into a *copla*, a folksong or light-hearted verse about the *pueblo* and its people. Or, to the rhythmic clapping of hands, couples would launch into a *sevillana*, the light-hearted *flamenco* dance that set the flounced skirts of the girls spinning merrily.

The *romería* was only the start. The *feria* went on for days. There were children's sports, clay pigeon-shooting, official balls, rock music, folk dancing, the big wheel, a roller-coaster, dodgems, shooting competitions and merry-go-rounds. But what there was most of all at the *feria* was talk and drinking and dancing. It was the social event of the year, when relatives came back to the *pueblo* and the womenfolk paraded their finery and father remembered he had a family and took them all out, no expense spared. You could get away with things in the *feria* that would have been impossible the rest of the year and many a marriage had its origins in tremulous moments in the velvety June night just beyond the reach of the fairground lights.

For a week the revelry went on until dawn. Or at least the noise did. Sheer cacophony was part of the fun; when your ear-drums threatened to explode and your chest cage went into spasms, you knew that you were really living it up. Each fairground attraction played a different tune at full blast, sirens howled, teenagers screamed on the dodgems and the ghost train, the bars redoubled their music volume to compete; *flamenco* and pop pounded out from the live entertain-ment arena, José launched rocket after rocket, and everybody talked twice as loud in order to be heard. There was no escaping the high-decibel inferno anywhere in the *pueblo*. But finally it ended, with an artillery barrage that sounded like the Battle of Trafalgar. Fireworks showered sparks across the night sky, filled the air with gunpowder fumes, and the *feria* was over.

Summer arrived in earnest after that. The heat built up and when it reached its breathless height in August, the summer visitors came. They wandered up from the coast, shamelessly displaying burnt flesh, peering into our doorways, and snapping picture after picture. The biggest invasion was of family. They came from Madrid and Barcelona and further afield, all those who had emigrated from the *pueblo* in the bad times, in the years of hunger when there were no jobs and the only way to survive was tramp up to the sierras and spend 16 hours chopping pine trees and bringing the trunks down on your mule's back or on your own. Some of those who made the annual pilgrimage home arrived in flashy cars and wore expensive clothes. They walked with a certain swagger and adopted the patronising air of sophisticated city-dwellers visiting under-privileged country cousins. Though, truth to say, there was not much sophistication about.

Amid emotional reunions and cheerful greetings, the population virtually doubled. The migrants brought their children and in-laws too, and they all squeezed into the homes of those who had stayed in the *pueblo*. There were so many relatives in Inocencia's house she had to sleep on the floor. She complained, but she accepted the situation fatalistically. After all, it was family. They came for a month, they paid no rent and contributed little to the food bill, but she did not mind shopping, cooking and cleaning for them. That was what mothers were for, even 75-year-old mothers.

Inocencia's life had been marked by tragedy. During the grim years when rebels had waged a vain guerrilla war against Franco's forces, she had lost a brother and her first husband in horrendous circumstances. Despite this and despite her age, she was indomitable, a small, tight-packed bundle of energy. She kept working into her 80s. When she was not slapping whitewash on a house, she was up a ladder painting a window frame or on hands and knees digging a garden. She did not know what holidays were.

Her nickname was La Caída (the fallen one). What story of village passion lay behind it, I wondered. It turned out that the name originated at a time when she ran a small bar on a narrow, steep street. So many customers tumbled down entering and especially leaving the establishment that the nickname "La Caída" was attached to her and her family ever afterwards.

Inocencia had impish bright eyes and an obscene turn of mind, as I discovered one day when she saw me carrying some tennis balls.

"What are those?" she asked and then broke into cackles. "They are pretty big for *cojones.*" It turned out that almost everything reminded Inocencia of *cojones.* You only had to mention "eggs" and she would be falling about the floor.

"Ay, I'll be glad when August is over and I can get my own bed back," she said one day. "I can't go to bed until all the family has come home because I sleep just inside the front door and they have to step over me. Then I have to get up at six every morning to prepare everybody's breakfast before I go off whitewashing."

But Inocencia was not really complaining. She would have been far sorer if the family had stayed away. While she toiled at her whitewashing, the family piled into their car and departed for long lazy days at the beach, returning with ravenous appetites and a load of dirty washing for *la abuela* (grandmother). Inocencia indulged them outrageously and gave all her whitewashing earnings to the children to buy chewing gum and sweets: "what would I do with the money? They're still young enough to enjoy it."

The summer heat sucked the last vestige of moisture out of the *campo* (countryside) and the energy out of everybody. On some days, suffocating blasts from Africa, from the Sahara itself, choked coast and sierras in dust, staining the sky an angry orange and streaking the village walls. Alcachofa, our sturdy neighbour, would come labouring up the street, exclaiming "*Ay, qué calor* (oh, what heat)" There was not much you could reply to that, except "*Sí, qué calor.*"

Like farmers everywhere, the local *campesinos* spent a good deal of time looking at the heavens and muttering. No matter what the weather, they could find portents of disaster in it. Most of all, and with reason, they muttered about water. Since no rain could be expected from May to October, only heavy winter rains could sustain the crops through to autumn, but the seasons had gone crazy, said the farmers, and often the rains were disappointing. During the long summer, black clouds might gather over the sierras and distant rumblings raise hopes, but the rain stayed away—or it came in a sudden cloudburst that ripped crops to pieces.

Every morning the irrigation custodian would climb up to the reservoir above the *pueblo* and fiddle with the sluices, directing the flow of water east or west, then redirecting it and splitting the flow as it hurried down the hillside along narrow channels. In spring the fields would receive water every two or three days, but in summer two weeks could pass, sometimes three, before a farmer's turn came to channel the flow into his tomato, pepper or melon patch. In bad years, the plants wilted, the leaves of the fruit trees browned at the edges, and the wells dried up.

Then it was that there were angry mutterings about the new villa-owners towards the coast with their fancy swimming pools. Sometimes, when the taps ran dry in the village, somebody would report they had seen one of the strangers—foreigners or *madrileños* (people from Madrid), it was all the same—refilling his pool just because the water had turned green. Sometimes when my shower produced less than a trickle, I would join in the muttering and dream of sabotaging all those lawn-sprinklers whirring day and night in the growing suburbia down the valley.

Water was a source of power and wealth and frequent dispute. Adolfo, a shrewd farmer with an eye to business, became the centre of one bitter conflict. He had found water on his land and generously offered to share it with all who wanted it, at a price. He sold millions of expensive litres, guaranteeing an annual supply. Pipes were laid to a score of properties that had previously only been able to support olive trees and vines. Their owners invested their savings in bulldozing new terraces, planting them with the exotic fruit trees that were fast becoming the rage, avocadoes, custard apples, loquats or mangoes. Newfangled drip irrigation caused the land to bloom, briefly. Then the drips grew fewer and smaller. Adolfo's greed had caught up with him, for there was simply not enough water to go around. He would have been lynched, if he could have been found. The desperate farmers had to seek new supplies before their properties reverted to desert.

But the arid heat of August was just what was needed to mature a traditional crop, luscious, plump Moscatel grapes. This was the month when the pickers started working their way laboriously up and down the steep hillsides and bunches of grapes appeared on every table. At night the pickers generally returned to the village and Antonio El Cronista, part-time archeologist and village historian, was full of nostalgia for the recent past when entire families spent the summer months at their farmhouses.

"Those are some of the best memories of my youth, out at the *cortijo* (farmhouse), when there were no roads, no radio, no television," he reminisced. "Adults and children, everybody, helped collect the grapes. It was hot and sweaty. But the nights were wonderful. We visited the other families or they would walk over to our place and we would sing and dance, by oil lamp or candles or under the moon. That was our entertainment, simple, traditional stuff. It's gone now, the songs are forgotten. A pity. We've lost something we can never regain."

On the hottest days, mountains, coast and *pueblo* steamed under a molten blanket of heat. The sun glinted on cars jamming the distant coastal highway and along the edge of the soup-like sea, on sands greasy with suntan lotion, the ranks of recumbent tourists rotated like sardines on a grill, spilling sweat and city cares. The tourists had their rituals, too.

A refreshing breeze might waft in from the sea along the coast, but in the *pueblo* the unrelenting heat paralysed thought and move-ment. In the houses, cool havens with the blinds and shutters closed, the families took long siestas or gazed, as in a stupor, at endless televi-sion soap operas. Down in the riverbed the boys frolicked all day in the reservoir, daring one another to plunge into the clear, weedy waters.

There was little relief at night, for the sea breezes did not reach the *pueblo*. Walls and cobbles gave out the heat they had stored by day. Long after midnight the villagers and their visiting relatives sat on doorsteps reminiscing endlessly, while the children skipped, or played football or hide and seek. On nights of full moon, when the shadows were as clear-cut as at midday, the cries of the children and the hum of talk reverberated through the streets until the early hours. After the doors had closed, the crickets and the frogs orchestrated their own chorus in the surrounding fields. Sometimes there would be a burst of *flamenco* singing and the staccato beating of palms as late-night rev-ellers rollicked home.

Then silence reigned, except when one last motor-cycle came howling through the *pueblo* to stir dogs and humans in their slumber.

8

A VINTAGE YEAR

It looked like being a vintage year. That, at least, is what I told myself every time I went into the stable. The mule had long gone, to be replaced by buckets of whitewash and garden tools. But it was not these that set my mouth watering and the flush of pride mounting to my cheeks. It was the rows of bottles nestling cosily in a corner, the product of months of study, toil and anxiety. There they sat, festooned with dust and cobwebs, full of that most noble of brews, one to make the Mouton-Rothschilds, the Lafites, and the rest of the snobbish clique stir uneasily in their four-poster beds. Yes, this was the home of Chateau Baird.

Summer had gone and tranquillity had returned to the *pueblo*. The relatives had bid tearful farewells, loaded themselves and innumerable packages into cars and buses and departed for another year. The heat lingered, but from one day to the next the *pueblo* was transformed. Even the light changed, from the harsh glitter of summer to the mellow glow of autumn. With a sigh of relief, the *pueblo* could resume normal life.

Trusty Ana, from across the street, often knocked on our door to present us with apronfuls of freshly-picked vegetables or fruit. I took a picture of her family and she inundated us with sweet green peppers, giant tomatoes, and avocadoes. Thea gave her flowers or a piece of ceramics and she turned up with custard apples and large, knobbly tubers, which proved to be delicious sweet potatoes. The villagers shipped many of the latter off to Estepa, a Seville town famous for its manufacture of sickly sweets. Year-round, Estepa smelled of Christmas candy.

In autumn, however, our *pueblo* was thick with another, more satisfying odour, that of fermenting grapes. On my first venture into the wine-making art, I did not feel confident enough to let on to the neighbours what I was up to in the stable. They were likely—to put it mildly—to be slightly sceptical. They had, after all, been at it for generations, using methods handed down from father to son since the time of the Romans; in the remoter farmhouses some still trod the grapes with their feet. The surrounding hillsides were testimony to their dedication to the grape. They spent months every year pruning, ploughing and fertilising or spraying.

Just before harvest time, everybody would prepare the large oak barrels, burning sulphur in them to get rid of any infectious organisms that could harm the fermenting must. As the grapes were picked, they were laid out on *paseros*, south-facing drying beds where the hot sun soon converted them into raisins, some of the most luscious raisins I have ever tasted. The grapes that went to the wine press were a mixture of the newly-picked and the sun-dried so their sugar content, and therefore the alcoholic content, would be high. You could taste the sunshine in that fruity Málaga wine.

My neighbours' knowledge came by word of mouth and experience handed down over the centuries. Mine came mostly from Boots the Chemist, which was why I kept a rather low profile. Boots, in fact, laid the foundations for Chateau Baird. To aid hard-up British alcoholics, their stores offered dozens of products for the do-it-yourself wino. Walking through one such store, I asked myself why—as one living amid countless hectares of vineyards—I had never ventured into this wine-making business. I bought a book on the art, a jar of all-purpose yeast, and a hydrometer (all wine-makers need one of these, the book assured me) and headed back to the sunshine. I could also have bought cans of concentrated grape juice and bags of corks, but scornfully rejected the idea. Good heavens, Spain was swimming in grape juice and cork literally grows on trees.

It was my first mistake. For several hours I tramped around the city of Málaga trying to find somebody who sold corks. In vain. There used to be a factory, I was told, but it had closed. Now the *bodegas* bought their corks by the thousand from distant producers.

Perhaps I was being a bit premature, I reflected. As yet there was no wine to bottle. I decided to forget about corks for a while. At least the *mosto*, grape juice, should be no trouble. The harvest was in full swing. The whole village reeked of rich, pungent, fruity juice fermenting in hidden vats, while mules loaded with freshly picked grapes queued up at the pressing mill. No problem here.

"*Mosto?*" Jaime, the mill owner, shook his head. "I'll ask, but most people only grow enough for their own use."

I tried Miguel.

"If only you'd said last week when I was picking."

Antonio was apologetic.

"I always have some left over. But not this year—it's been a poor harvest. Try Don Sebastian."

Don Sebastian was the biggest landowner. His vineyards ran

on for ever. But he was a joyless soul. As old and withered as one of his own vines, he sat in his funeral suit in the darkest corner of his kitchen. At my question, he shrank back into the shadows.

"*Mosto?*" His voice was like two twigs being rubbed together. "None to spare, none to spare."

Finally, just when it seemed as though my hopes of competing with Mouton-Rothschild and company were to be squashed at birth, I found a supplier who was having his grapes processed at the press. His bloodshot eyes and general unsteadiness suggested that I had found another connoisseur. He loaded two 16-litre glass containers, known as *arrobas*, of muddy-looking juice on his mule and, weaving an erratic route, transported them to my house. Because the stuff was in short supply, the price was two to three times that of the previous year. It looked as though my wine was going to be more expensive than good-quality Rioja.

Never mind. It was quality that counted. I pressed on. My book assured me that as I was only handling a relatively small quantity it was wiser to use glass containers rather than barrels for fermentation. Small casks allow too much air to get to the wine because their ratio of surface area to volume was too great and over-exposure to air, through the porous wood, will harm the wine. That made sense. Also I did not own a barrel. But how was I to explain this to my neighbours? Whoever heard of making wine in glass bottles? They already thought I was rather eccentric. Best to keep this wine-making under cover.

I became even more furtive when tackling the fermentation technique since my book was not in accord with local methods. Natural yeast on the grape-skins set up a lively fermentation lasting six to eight weeks. As the wine cleared, it was decanted into another barrel and there was no nonsense about waiting for it to mellow. Within six months all the wine had either been sold or polished off. Only rarely would you find local wine more than a year old.

The wine was prized for its sweetness and heaviness but I wanted to produce a drier variety, which meant keeping the *mosto* fermenting until all the sugar had been converted into alcohol. The first

task, according to the book, was to suppress the wild yeast and kill off any micro organisms which might convert the wine to vinegar or worse. So I added some organism-killing sulphite tablets to the must and prepared my imported yeast separately.

Twenty-four hours later, however, something seemed to have gone wrong. The wild yeast was fizzing away furiously, as though in protest at the killer sulphite tablets, while the fancy stuff from Boots in its "starter bottle" appeared to have given up the ghost. Guiltily remembering the locals' frequent boast that their wine was "pure and without chemicals", I tossed in some more sulphite and tried to infuse more life into the bottle of yeast. It was hopeless. Nothing was working like the book said.

In desperation, I tossed the comatose yeast into the angry must and sat back to await results, after carefully fitting an air-lock on each *arroba*. My book said it was most essential to use this device to avoid infection by fruit flies and other noxious influences. It was comforting to know that all this modern technology was on my side. The locals, poor souls, had no such advantages. They had never heard of air-locks. They just put a slate over the hole in the barrel.

The juice bubbled briskly away, but it was not as lively as I had expected. I consulted books and do-it-yourself experts. They advised me that the temperature in the stable was probably too low. Good fermentation demanded a warmer environment. Late one night, after the neighbours had gone to bed, I sneaked into the stable and made several unsteady journeys back to the house under the weight of the wine containers. Delicately planted in the spare bedroom, they emitted a steady series of burps. I dozed off, dreaming blissfully of the yeast working away at converting the sugar into alcohol that soon became Niagaras of sparkling wine. A few hours later I awakened, shaken by violent sneezing. The sneezing would not stop and I realised that I was slowly being poisoned by the carbon dioxide from the wine.

Fortunately the moon had set as I began staggering back to the stable with the *arrobas*, a journey that involved negotiating the rough cobbles in the street. One slip would have been disastrous and I could not imagine what story would have satisfied the neighbours had I been discovered carrying about containers of fermenting wine at 3am.

The feeble invalid in the stable was taking up more of my time than I had anticipated. Hoping to encourage the patient's fermentation, I took to carrying it on to the patio so that it could be warmed by the sun, then back inside when the sun went down. Wine-making was proving much harder work than I had envisaged.

Soon, the rest of the village was tossing back gallons of newly-matured wine. I checked mine every day, but it just went on burping irritatingly slowly.

Just to encourage me, it turned out to be a bad year. The wine was turning out paler than usual, with less flavour, and it was reluctant to clarify.

"It's the weather," insisted one villager. "The summer was too damp."

"It's that new mechanical press," said another. "Next time it's back to the feet."

My book said nothing about the dangers of using mechanical presses. It had plenty of other information, though, about the dangers to new wine, making it sound more fragile than a young baby. There were dozens of afflictions that could destroy the fermentation. It might have too much tannin, too much iron, too much pectin, too little tartaric acid. It could be stricken by acetification, metallic casse, flowers of wine, pousse, tourne, mildew . . . the list was endless and the cures mind-boggling, from adding chalk to pumping in glycerine. It did not sound like the sort of wine I wanted to make at all.

"Is that right you're making wine?" asked Jaime, "I'll have to come over and try some. Still fermenting? Strange. Well, you must watch out for one thing. Don't let a woman in the same room if she's having her period. It'll turn the wine off for sure."

My book did not mention that one, oddly enough. At last the must stopped fermenting. On sampling, it proved to be sweeter than I had hoped though the alcoholic content was up near 17 per cent. I tried to start it fermenting again, putting in more yeast. More heat was obviously needed so once again I made the furtive journey from stable to house, this time arraying the containers in front of the living-room fire. My efforts were fruitless, however. The burping had stopped for good.

I decanted the wine and checked the colour. It looked good, warm, golden, user-friendly. I tasted it. Yes, well, maybe it should rest a while, for a couple of weeks at least. I sampled it again a few weeks later to see if there was any change, any progress. I sampled it frequently. It was not bad, not bad at all; without presumption but palatable. In fact, it tasted very similar to... er... well to my neighbours' wine. All that effort and you could not tell the difference. So much for modern technology. Perhaps the answer was to let it mature. That was surely the answer.

A couple of months later the wine had cleared well and the visit of two friends provided the occasion for some more serious sampling. They knocked off a bottle between them while I contented myself with a glassful. They left in high spirits, undeterred by the prospect of driving along the tortuous coast road to Almería. I often wonder what happened to them. I do know that for the next day or so our bathroom got a good deal more use than usual.

Obviously more maturing was needed. That was what the book said. Rack into a new container to remove the lees and leave for two to three months, then check again. That was the secret of quality. You could not hurry it.

Bottling the first year's production of Chateau Baird was quite an event in its way. In years to come I could imagine some of those bottles coming up at Sotheby's. "Chateau-bottled," they would say, "One of the great years. A collector's item."

I don't know though. When I checked the stable some time later, something odd was happening. Those Boots corks that had taken me hours to hammer into the bottles were popping out like cannon balls. I picked up my wine bible to seek an explanation. Then I had second thoughts and went in search of Jaime.

9

THE MIRACLE

Early one morning we took the old road to Granada. It lay just behind the *pueblo*, a rocky path that looped and zig-zagged over the hills and was now sadly overgrown. Once it had been travelled by the *arrieros*, a bunch of men who dedicated themselves to rushing fish to Granada markets from the Mediterranean. In the evening they would wait on the beaches for the returning fishermen, load their mules with up to 200 kilos of newly-caught fish, then set off into the interior.

The path was treacherous enough by day. On a dark night it must have been a truly hazardous journey as it skirted precipitous gorges and scaled a pass 2000 feet above sea level. The muleteers travelled at a brisk walk or even a run, encouraging their animals, the biggest, strongest brutes they could find, to greater efforts. Several *ventas*, primitive wayside inns, dotted the route. Approaching one of these, a muleteer would slap his animal's rump to encourage it on its way, stride inside, swig back the *aguardiente* the innkeeper had waiting and, with barely a pause, continue out the other door to rejoin his mule. Speed was essential: if they missed the morning market they would be stuck with a load of fast-decomposing fish.

Motor transport changed the picture. But even after the Civil War, that benchmark in Spanish history, mule-trains continued to wend their way through the sierras, carrying flour, olive oil and other commodities. It was a grim time of serious shortages and the *contra-bandistas* flourished, slipping along remote trails to evade police controls.

For our excursion to Granada, we left when darkness still enveloped the *pueblo*. We paused to buy bread at the bakery, then joined the men and their mules setting out for the fields. At first the track wound past the cultivated terraces, then climbed into foothills clad with vines, almond and olive-trees. It was an enchanted morning. The rising sun dissolved the mists over a mercury-smooth sea and brushed with indigo the tips of the limestone crags thrusting up from the dark valleys to our north. Water tumbling along the irrigation channels rang in our ears and a distant farmhouse sent a thin column of smoke into the early stillness.

Around a bend two Civil Guards lay in wait. Olive-green sentinels with tricorn hats and impassive faces, they sat on a rock, puffing cigarettes. They watched our progress, showing little interest but registering our every detail.

"Granada?" They raised their eyebrows. "Up there. But the track is bad. Nobody goes that way any more."

As we trudged on, we passed beneath the great 4000-feet-high bulk of El Fuerte. On those barren heights, when the manic-obsessive King Philip 11 was carrying out his Catholic crusade, persecuted descendants of the Moors had fought and lost a desperate battle. Whitened bones and bits of armour still turned up on El Fuerte's scarred slopes. We passed beneath an ochre-hued cliff where Moors fleeing Christian armour had tossed over chickens to see if they would survive the drop. Seeing that the birds landed safely, the Moors proceeded to jump, unhappily with less satisfactory results.

Amid the scent of pines, we passed an abandoned hamlet, a relic of a later conflict. The story went that the inhabitants had fled their homes when they found themselves caught between two fires during the guerrilla war of the 1940s. In a desperate attempt to overthrow the dictator, the Communists had organised rebel groups in the sierras, one of which had operated in the mountains behind the *pueblo*. They had been violent, hungry years, which had touched every family. Memories of that era were etched deep, but there was a reluctance to talk about them, as though they were too horrible to contemplate.

All day we walked deeper into the sierra. Lizards skittered away at our passing and a snake, sunning itself on the path, slid harmlessly into the undergrowth. Disturbed from its slumbers, a *cabra montés* charged out of a rocky gully and disappeared into the scrub. In drier seasons these wild goats would sneak down to the village to nibble plants in gardens and fields, but there were not many left, thanks to forest fires and poachers. We saw few signs of human activity. Apart from the ruins of the old *ventas*, here and there were circular pits walled with rocks, where limestone was baked to produce the whitewash for the *pueblo*. A lone goatherd watching over his flock on a distant hilltop raised a hand in salute. At midday, in a valley brittle with silence, we paused to bathe in a rock pool formed by a cascading stream. Hawks wheeled lazily overhead.

Then, under a hammering sun, we climbed and sweated up through the pine trees and juniper and tumbled boulders to El Puerto, the pass that led to Granada. This was the old road to Granada. This was the way the *arrieros* had come night after night. This was where earlier this century the *bandoleros*, highwaymen, had ruled and robbed. This was where the rebels had fought and dodged Franco's men for years, sleeping in caves or in the open in all seasons. Whatever the men of the sierras were driven by, hunger, greed, fear, or ideals, they were a breed apart.

One of the *arrieros*, Miguel, a frail and withered shadow in his 90s, had told me about the rigours of his nightly trek through the mountains in the early years of this century.

"It was tough enough in summer, but it was worse in winter when it could be snowing up there on the Puerto. There would be ice on the track and rivers in flood. We had beautiful mules. They were so big and strong they stood out, like a Mercedes among cars today. But they never lasted long. After a few years they were burned out. Their legs would go or they would die on the track, and some were washed away with their owners when they tried to cross one of the torrents."

"*Hombre*, but it was hard. My feet used to hurt so much. But you had to keep moving or you would be late at market and nobody would want your fish. Even if prices were low, you had to sell your load to raise cash for the next trip. You could work two days and have nothing to show for it. But it was better than working the land. There was no money in that."

There had been outlaws too, to keep the muleteers on their toes. Miguel recalled being held up by two ruffians with shotguns and paying them off with four big fish. The heyday of highwaymen and smugglers was last century, when for a while they ruled the sierras of Andalusia. The smuggler, according to Richard Ford, illustrious pioneer of English travel writers, was welcome in every village: "He is the newspaper and channel of intelligence, bringing tea and gossip for the curate, money and cigars for the attorney, ribands and cotton for the women."

Ford warned travellers that "the absence of a watch can only be accounted for by a premeditated intention of not being robbed of it," which could seriously upset any *bandoleros* encountered en route.

Washington Irving, the American diplomat who publicised Granada's wonders, travelled with "a little surplus of hard dollars by way of a robber purse to satisfy the gentlemen of the road should we be assaulted".

Irving and Ford did much to create a romantic halo about the 19th century outlaws. There were numerous tales about these to support the romantic image. One concerned our *pueblo*. A priest once arrived at the mansion where the big landowner's agent lived and asked to see him. Once in his presence, he produced a gun from under his cassock, demanded all the agent's valuables and then forced him to escort him past the Civil Guards to the edge of the village, where he leapt on a horse and escaped.

In fact, most of the *bandoleros* would not have recognised Robin Hood if he had hit them over the head with his quarter staff. Some men turned outlaw through desperation at injustice and hunger, but gallantry was in short supply among those cut-throats. They created a reign of terror, robbing, kidnapping, and killing for the pleasure of it. The *pueblo*'s doctor was one of their victims.

Chivalry was not a word that came to mind when talking of El Bizco, for example. A colleague of the fake priest, he was one of the most notorious outlaws in our zone in the 1880s. To judge by contemporary accounts and his pictures, there was precious little romance about him. In fact, El Bizco was the stuff of nightmares, cross-eyed, brutish of feature, with sadistic tastes. Erupting into isolated communities, he liked victims to plead for mercy and kiss his blunderbuss. "He was more beast than man, capable of the worst cruelties," reported a commander of the Civil Guard, a force that was created in response to the widespread banditry. El Bizco killed six Guards and at least two peasants. While he and his gang were still on the run, they were sentenced to death by the garrote, but El Bizco escaped that fate. He was finally cornered and shot.

When we had finally struggled to the top of the pass, we looked down on a gentler landscape. Pine forests dropped away into the distance towards fields of wheat and barley. We walked more swiftly on the descent into Granada province, pausing occasionally to watch the trout playing in a stream. Earthenware receptacles hung on many of the pine trees to catch dripping resin. The forest gave way to fields of wheat and barley, speckled with poppies, and at evening, exhausted, we collapsed into sleeping bags on the shores of a reservoir.

The villages on this side of the mountains, not blessed by a year-round mild climate, unvisited by tourists, proved to be poorer and more primitive than ours. Even so, we were not prepared for the miracle. It appeared that in one of the villages, the smallest, the remotest and the poorest of all, a woman had been cured of tuberculosis after the doctors had given her up. And the cure had come overnight, after a strange visitation.

Hidden in a fold of the sierras, the village was a miserable enough place, a mere cluster of houses with only a handful of inhabitants. Don Saturnino, the village priest, was eager to talk about the miraculous event, more than eager. Thickset and white-haired, he was a stern, unyielding man of God who ruled his flock with a rod of iron.

"Here the people do not seek luxuries," he told us. "They have simplicity and weakness in their poverty. The women keep their arms covered and always wear plain clothing instead of wasting their money on modern fashions. Thus it is that they have more time to think about the Lord."

And what of the miracle?

"Ah, that is what it is, indeed," he said, fingering his rosary. "Margarita was sick for years from tuberculosis. She was weak and vomited blood. The specialists said her left lung was 90 per cent destroyed and the right lung was also injured. For 15 years she was ill, yet in less than five minutes she was restored. There is not even a scar on her lungs. The doctors cannot explain it scientifically. They say it's an amazing case. Yes, it's a miracle."

The priest said he would take us to Margarita's house and we accompanied him along the street. Small boys ran up to greet him, kissing the ringed hand he extended. It was an old custom that had died out elsewhere, but not in Don Saturnino's domain.

"Margarita is not at home, but you can see her room," said the priest, leading us upstairs. The priest pressed a switch and dozens of light bulbs illuminated the scene. The ceiling had been panelled in pine and a large altar, bearing statues of the Virgin, filled one corner.

"There is her bed," said Don Saturnino.

He indicated a thick wooden plank. Nails had been hammered into it in the shape of a cross and the pillow was a wooden log. A heavy wooden cross leaned against the wall by the bed. It was not your ordinary bedroom and we looked a little blankly at the priest.

He smiled in satisfied fashion.

"I shall explain Margarita's saintly life. She sleeps very little. At 11 o'clock every night she kneels down on that board, yes, that one covered with nails, and stays there praying for five hours for the sinners and unfaithful.

"On Fridays she gives herself some lashes with that barbed wire whip, then she puts on a hair shirt and makes the Via Crucis, carrying the cross up and down. Sometimes she falls down, because it is heavy for her."

We gazed in awe at the cross and the nailed bed.

"At night," went on the priest, "Margarita never has more than a glass of milk and a small piece of bread and for breakfast she has coffee without sugar. She went once for a year without drinking water, which would normally be impossible to endure."

Father Saturnino sighed.

"It's a life of penance. But if God has ordered it then clearly she must try to do it for He does not order the impossible. Hers is a life of sacrifice. She prays particularly for the priests, sacrificing herself so that the priests who have turned aside from God return to their path."

He looked around with pride at the nailed bed, the panelled ceiling and the cross.

"I made all this. I used to be a carpenter before taking up the priesthood," he said.

Margarita proved to be a plump, contented-looking lady, undistinguished in any way. Her centre-parted hair was dark brown with no sign of grey, although she was in her 50s. She talked in a relaxed, matter-of-fact way about her experiences.

"I still can't believe how well I feel after all those years when I could hardly climb the stairs. Why, I could barely walk or breathe. The doctors made tests and said there was nothing they could do for me."

"Then one night a great light filled my room, and another night I was visited by the Virgin Mary. She told me to say rosaries for the Pope and the priests and all sinners. That's what I did and then the Lord himself appeared to me. It was about 10.30 one night. I spoke to Him and He appeared to be of real flesh and blood. He said He was going to cure me and He made the sign of the Cross over my chest and shoulders and I felt a tremendous force inside me. I felt the weight of the Lord's hands, a normal contact, like yours or anyone else's. He asked me to pray and make sacrifices."

Margarita emanated good health and conviction.

"I felt better immediately and soon afterwards I went to the doctor and asked him to examine me. He did X-rays, but he could find nothing wrong. He was absolutely astonished. The tuberculosis had disappeared. Today I'm perfectly healthy. The Lord cured me. It's a miracle. There can be no doubt about that."

Father Saturnino had no doubts either. He showed copies of impressive-looking certificates in which doctors testified that all traces of the tuberculosis, for which they had unsuccessfully treated Margarita, had disappeared.

"I have given all the documents, the medical certificates and the rest, to the bishop. There should be a full investigation so that this case can be officially declared a miracle."

We walked back slowly over the sierras. All the way back to the *pueblo*, I thought of Saturnino striding through his village and the boys running up to kiss his hand. But most of all I thought of Margarita, so sweet and trusting, and her bed of nails.

10

A MATTER OF FATE

For some events in the *pueblo* there was no explanation, or none that seemed logical at least. Take the case of the blocked pipe.

One morning a stain no larger than a man's hand appeared on our kitchen wall. By lunchtime, it was pumpkin-proportioned. By next morning it was the size of a baby elephant. It was time to call a plumber. I knew people who had called plumbers. A pathetic lot they were. They would weep on your shoulder in abject fashion, insisting on recounting absurdly exaggerated stories. Some had changed houses by the time the plumber arrived. Others had remarried, changed jobs, travelled three times around the world, and retired, and they were still waiting.

One friend tried for months to have a simple repair job done. He met the plumber every day, as he lived close by, and they always exchanged cheerful greetings.

"*Qué tal, Aurelio?*" he would say. "When are you coming to fix that pipe?"

Aurelio would smile and apologise. He was very busy.

"Can't make it today. But tomorrow for sure. Ten o'clock? I'll be there."

He never was. After six months or so, my friend, a fellow of considerable resource and ingenuity, took extreme measures. He went to the post office and sent a telegram to Aurelio: "Urgent. Come immediately."

The next morning (telegrams moved with considerable speed in our *pueblo*) there was a pounding at the front door. Aurelio was

there, wide-eyed, clutching the telegram.

"I've never had one of these before. What's happened? Are you ill?"

I did not send a telegram, but something had to be done fast as the stain on the wall had swelled from a small elephant to a jumbo. I knew not to call Emilio. He had responded to a previous emergency. After examining a large damp spot, he had looked at me in surprise and asked what the problem was.

"It looks as though that connection you put in is leaking through the plaster."

"That's true," he had replied. "But that's normal. Joints usually leak."

This time I put my faith in José Manuel, a keen young fellow who set to work with a will. He smashed through our kitchen wall for several hours, tracing the path of the waste pipe. Finally, he emerged triumphantly from the debris and held out his hand.

"The drain was blocked. With this."

I stared at the cause of our troubles, an intact electric light bulb. An electric light bulb!

"But how? How could that get into the waste pipe from the kitchen sink?"

He shrugged.

"Maybe it's a gift from heaven."

Why not? The good Lord was responsible for almost everything in the *pueblo*. The words "*Si Dios quiere* (if God wills it)" or "*Gracias a Dios*" were tagged on to almost every statement, prediction, or promise. "See you tomorrow, if God wills it," "Everything will work out, if God wills it" . . . It was easy to believe that the Moors had once been here. All was in the hands of Allah. He controlled our destinies. He brought the blessing of rain and He brought the curse of floods. If something went wrong, it was His will. Divine providence ruled and you could not fight it.

He was not a very benevolent deity to judge by the number of accidents that sprinkled village life. Everywhere you looked there was somebody on crutches or with an arm in a sling, caused by unprovoked attacks by inanimate objects. Apparently possessed by the devil, these objects regularly tripped up people, ran away with them, or ran over them. The earth moved and tossed people down ravines, scaffolding disintegrated, machines rose in revolt. With amazing frequency the road to the coast—a malevolent piece of work if ever there was one—picked up cars and motor-cycles and tossed them into potato fields.

"It was that accursed curve. There should be guard rails. The straight stretch caught me unawares. There are no warning signs. It's a scandal. The wheel leaped out of my hands. The brakes didn't work. The tree just came up and hit me."

The narrow road was particularly sneaky after midnight. That was when it would tweak the handle-bars of youthful models of sobriety carefully negotiating its bends after a sedate visit to the disco and launch them into eternity.

Buses and trains were mischievous, too. When somebody missed one, it was not because he was tardy. "The bus escaped me," was a common expression. Nobody dropped anything; instead, "*se me cayó*" (literally, it fell from me). You didn't lose an object: "*se me perdió la bolsa*" (the bag, of its own volition and without my permission, lost me).

These incidents were not something over which an individual had any control. They were clearly pre-ordained. This was very convenient. Who could be held responsible for the vagaries of fate and the uncontrolled movements of mischievous objects and other humans? More importantly, this fatalism sustained the villagers through the hardships and sorrows that had always been a part of daily life. It was an attitude that had been formed over centuries in a peasant community at the mercy at one time or another of pirates, warlords, distant monarchs, capricious aristocrats, unscrupulous politicians, and unthinking bureaucrats.

Forty years of dictatorship had only entrenched the conviction that it was safest to bear the whims of fate with stoic patience and never to meddle with authority. With luck an *enchufe*, a contact with influence, might intercede on one's behalf, but otherwise there was little to be done. Accepting that the course of events was inevitable helped one come to terms with tragedy and injustice. The wise man did not ask questions: he kept his head down and played whatever cards were dealt him.

Adelina, a robust woman in her 30s, tripped and broke her leg. She sat in her house, white with pain and shock, as a fluttering of housewives wailed and wept over her misfortune, until somebody thought of calling an ambulance. It had to come from the next town and it was two hours before she was carried down the steep street and borne off to hospital, a journey of an hour and a half. Ten days went by and then they brought Adelina home, in a coffin. They had fixed her leg in hospital, but somehow a clot had formed in her blood stream. It had travelled to her brain and killed her. Her husband and children were overcome with grief and the whole village went into shock. She had been so strong and goodhumoured. How could it be?

The lamentations were loud and heart-rending.

"How awful! The poor soul! How sad for the family! It's not fair. May she rest in peace."

Adelina went to her grave and life went on. No proper explanation of her death was forthcoming. There was no inquest. Nobody thought of asking for one. It was the way things were, the will of God.

On occasions such as this, it was hard to accommodate oneself to the immobility of *pueblo* thinking. But, if you were born in the village, it took a strong character to go against the rigid code that ruled every phase of existence. When I first came to the *pueblo*, I found that one of the words most frequently on my lips was one rarely used by the locals—"Why?" Why were front doors painted brown and ceilings green? Why did the farmers always sell to middle-men even though they knew they were being ripped off? Why did they plant potatoes when the prices were so bad? Why did you eat 12 grapes as the clock chimed the first minutes of the New Year? Why did women go to Mass but not the men? Why could a woman never go out unless accompanied by her husband? Why did sons laze around while their sisters did all the housework?

The answer was always the same.

"It's the custom."

If you phrased the question differently, there was an alternative, even more conclusive reply.

"It's not the custom."

Few were ready to challenge such a code, least of all young Purísima. She was a gentle, soft-eyed innocent, but she had sinned and that was that. It had happened so easily. Manolo was tall and strong, and persuasive. He was 25 and he knew much about the world and its ways. Somehow the two of them had evaded family vigilance. It may have happened only once or twice, but that had been enough. Purísima panicked when she started suffering morning sickness. There was nobody to turn to, except the priest. He listened to her confession and said she must tell her parents. Her father was furious, her mother in tears. But everybody knew what had to be done. The couple must get married. There was no other way out.

Manolo shrugged his shoulders and fulfilled his duty. The gilt-edged invitations went out with the inscription followed as usual by the initials DM (*Dios manda*, God willing). God apparently gave his approval, for Purísima duly married in white, as custom demanded. The priest overlooked her youth, the ceremony was performed, and the families tried their best to carry it off in the proper style, with a feast that outshone many another *pueblo* wedding.

Shortly afterwards, Purísima felt the first birth pains. They took her to hospital and a small but healthy child was born. But it was a difficult birth because of the girl's small stature. After all, the age of 13 is rather young to start a family. Purísima was little more than an infant and she haemorrhaged badly. Nothing the doctors did could staunch the blood. Her life ebbed away.

If there was remorse, not everybody shared it. One relative gave his moral judgment: "The girl should never have run around with a man that age. She acted like a *puta* (whore). It's sad that she died, but God willed it. It is His punishment."

The bedroom where they laid the diminutive coffin was filled with weeping mourners. Purísima's mother collapsed across the coffin, her shoulders heaving with her hysterical sobbing for hour after hour.

"*Ay, mi hija! Mi hija!* My daughter! My daughter!"

From the family and friends rose cries of "*Pobrecita!* (poor little one)" and "What a pity!" and "What a tragedy!" The wailing and moans of grief reached such an intensity that the very room seemed to vibrate. In its way, it served as a catharsis for the pain and the guilt of Purísima's death.

Hallowed ritual took charge of the funeral details. The women did not go to the cemetery, as it was not the custom. The coffin was walled up in the family niche. Outside the gates, the males of the family lined up to receive condolences. The mourners shook hands with each of them, uttering the usual words: "*En paz descanse.* May she rest in peace. *En paz descanse.*" And Purísima's father, brothers, uncles replied: "*Que Dios se lo pague.* May God reward you."

There remained the problem of the motherless child, but that was soon resolved. It was decided that the baby should be looked after by Manolo's parents. He was free to seek another wife. It had been a bad time, but he was consoled by the knowledge that he had done the honourable thing and acquitted himself as an *hombre* should. As custom demanded, in fact.

11

EXECUTION AT DAWN

Guillermo's knife had been sharpened so often it was like a Gillette blade. He honed it on a smooth stone, sweeping it backwards and forwards in rhythmic, practised movements until the edge was so keen that it felt dangerous even to walk in front of it. It matched its owner, for if ever a man fitted the image of one who was licensed to kill it was Guillermo. He was built like an executioner, a big man, thickset, with a thin smile on his lips below an even thinner, black moustache. No doubt he shaved with the deadly tool of his craft.

He came striding out of the mists at dawn, stamping up and down the terrace of the *cortijo*, the thin moustache twitching. He sank a glass of *aguardiente*, refusing another, and—caressing his knife—asked: "Where is he then? It's time to get started."

The shrill cries of the victim slashed through the early morning stillness as he was dragged protesting across the farm living-room and on to the verandah. By some intuition he must have known what was in store for him. And he could have had no doubt when he saw Guillermo waiting, with his knife. Funny how executions are always at dawn.

Not that it seemed too funny at the time. Guillermo and his murderous blade somehow did not fit into the picture of rural bliss that I had conjured up when Antonio had first invited me to spend a weekend in the country. It was December and his friend Manolo *de Los Cuatro Vientos*, the one who lived in the magnificent *cortijo* on the crest of a hill, was due to slaughter a fine pig that had been fattening for months. We could all stay the night and join the feast next day.

Images, mouth-watering images, flicked through my mind, lifted I later realised from some old painting of rustic jollification. A whole pig turning slowly over blazing olive logs as rosy-cheeked children dance around, hot pork fat dropping sizzling into the flames, the tender, juicy meat flavoured with garlic and wild thyme, laughing countryfolk sampling the host's wine matured in oak barrels in the cobwebbed cool of his ancient farmhouse. The simple rural life at its best. We bundled up our sleeping bags and prepared to go.

Even though Antonio assured me that there would be no shortage of sleeping accommodation, I also took along two collapsible camp beds for myself and Thea. Some sixth sense told me that the simple country life was not all featherbeds and *fino*. We plodded out of the *pueblo*, Antonio leading his mule, the rest of us following behind. A narrow, rocky track led into the hills. The path snaked up a narrow gully, where cactuses leaned out drunkenly from the sides as though about to collapse and skewer us to the rock.

It was a tough climb. Just as we reached the top, a woman in her 50s came striding along. In one hand she carried a basket, in the other an umbrella, and on her feet she wore carpet slippers. She gazed at us curiously as we came panting up the slope.

"Where are you going?" she asked, with the usual directness of *pueblo* folk. At first I used to take such questions seriously and answer in precise detail. But that, as Antonio demonstrated, was not playing the game correctly.

"*Pues... arriba,*" he said.

She studied the laden mule, Antonio's family and the extranjeros.

"To see Fernando the Lame One, then?"

"Fernando? His wife's in hospital, you know."

"It's late to go to the *cortijo.*"

"True."

"Just for a walk then?"

"You could say that."

"It will be dark soon."

"In a couple of hours. And you? To the *pueblo*?"

"*Sí*. To the *pueblo*. You'll be coming back tonight, I suppose?"

"Ah, well, it depends. *Bueno*. We're going. *Adiós*."

"*Vaya con Dios*."

You could see her pondering as she continued on her way. Puzzling out where Antonio and his band were going would keep her entertained all the way back to the *pueblo*, where she would discuss the question with everybody she met, until the truth came out.

It was almost night before we reached Manolo's place and the damp winter weather set me thinking about mulled wine and cosy farmhouse hospitality. Manolo was in good spirits, indeed he seemed to be soaked in them. He smiled broadly, revealing a single decayed tooth and beckoned us inside. His wife, as serenely beautiful as her husband was impishly ugly, was tending an open fire, but "cosy" was not the first word to spring to mind when describing their abode. Crates of raisins were piled on the concrete floor of the living room.

"The prices were so bad this year that I refused to sell the raisins. It was plain robbery," explained Manolo, "I'm waiting until the market improves."

As there were no chairs in sight, we sat on the crates. Furniture was confined to a rickety table. A few pots and pans were lodged on shelves near the hearth, but Manolo had not done much in the way of decor. Unless you counted the calendar nailed on the wall. It featured a green fishing net from behind which leered a naked, brown-eyed blonde of amazing proportions. Even that however did not raise the temperature of the room. It felt chilly despite the fire and I began to harbour worries about the sleeping accommodation.

Manolo, at least, was free with his wine. He poured out large measures for everybody and an even bigger one for himself. He watched closely as I took a large gulp of the amber liquid. It was not the best wine. That was the first thing you had to admit. It was definitely not good wine. It was not mediocre wine either. It was not even

bad wine. It was terrible wine. In fact, it was without doubt the worst wine I had ever tasted. And that, from a plonk artist of many years' standing, is saying something.

Manolo gave me a toothy grin.

"Good, eh?"

Smiling when your mouth has been scoured with vinegar is not an easy task but I just about managed it. I was unable to speak.

"Have some more," said Manolo, draining his own glass, smacking his lips and refilling the glasses.

Antonio, I noticed, had set down his glass and was grimacing.

"*Hombre*, when did you make this?" he asked.

"I picked the grapes a while back," said Manolo cheerfully, "Let me see. Yes, it started fermenting three or four weeks ago. It's still a bit cloudy but just right for drinking."

He produced a jar.

"Try my olives."

I tasted one, gingerly. Holy smoke! It was worse than the wine.

"There's something wrong with these," said Antonio.

"Surely not," said Manolo, "I picked them last week."

He chewed a couple, nodding his head in appreciation and swilling them down with his three-week-old wine. Supper was tomatoes, stale bread and stringy sausage. We all chewed steadily, as a cold wind from the sierras tugged at the broken tiles in the roof. Not for nothing was Manolo's place known as Los Cuatro Vientos.

It turned out that the sleeping facilities were a little less grandiose than he had promised. Indeed, by the time Antonio and his wife and three children had slotted themselves into the two available beds, there was nothing left for anyone else. Congratulating ourselves on our foresight, my wife and I proceeded to assemble our camp-beds, to the fascination and astonishment of our companions. Manolo took another shot of wine and stretched out on a mule blanket with his wife before the fireplace. His snores kept me awake for several hours, while a chill dampness rose from the bare concrete and gradually ate into my bone marrow.

With the grey first light came Guillermo and his knife. The pig, dragged from its sty somewhere beyond the only bedroom, was put to slow and agonising death. Guillermo slit its throat with his knife, then wiggled the knife about in the wound to make sure it bled well. My wife stuck her fingers in her ears and fled to the fields to escape the beast's last groans as its life-blood dripped into a bowl. Manolo's and Antonio's wives carried out bowls of scalding water to pour over the corpse so that Guillermo could strip away the bristles more easily. Then a scaffolding was erected for the dissection in the living room.

With precise surgical strokes, Guillermo began stripping away the flesh, removing the intestines for the making of blood sausages.

Manolo watched everything happily, occasionally warming himself with a glass of *anís*. It was a cool and overcast morning and dreams of hot coffee and bacon and eggs and croissants and toast and marmalade began to tantalise me. But nobody else seemed to be thinking of food, for no pause was made for breakfast. They all appeared to be fuelled up on *aguardiente*. Especially Manolo.

Unveiling his tooth, he suggested I take a picture of him, of his house, of his pig, of his children, and another, and another. . . Soon he had switched from *anís* to wine. He offered me some, crying "What a feast we're going to have!" Make it soon, I muttered to myself.

The children were dispatched into the surrounding country-side, bearing basketfuls of fresh meat for sale to the neighbours. The women began stuffing sausage skins. One of the village bakers trudged up leading his mule on his daily bread round to the farms. He accepted a glass of wine, gulped, and made a rapid departure. Midday was approaching, but there was no sign of breakfast, or lunch. No sign of roast pork, or barbecued pork, or grilled pork, or fried ham. Only olives tasting like quinine bullets and wine that could have been stolen from a Jumbo jet's fuel tanks.

But the banquet was coming. Guillermo knew his stuff. He carved and sliced expertly. He cut away fat for rendering down, chis-elled out juicy chops, carved out choice fillets. My mouth watered in anticipation. After the frugal supper of the previous evening, the long, cold night, and the fast since dawn, the prospect of best pork was over-whelming. It had to be a sumptuous meal.

I continued to believe that even as I watched the fillets carried to the hearth where a cauldron was simmering away. Before I could utter so much as a despairing cry, the fillets were chopped into small pieces and tossed into a gallon of olive oil. In too went onions, toma-toes, garlic, and what seemed like a kilo or two of saffron. The mixture was stirred frequently by Manolo's wife, who never stopped working. Manolo went on drinking.

Eventually, after an hour—or maybe it was two hours—of cooking, the cauldron was carried triumphantly outside. Armed with forks, we gathered around. Everybody tucked in, soaking slices of bread in the hot juice and pronging the lumps of meat floating in the greasy morass. The meat was tasty, as tasty as anything that has been boiled in oil, and as I ate it fantasies taunted me of how it would have been if it had been sliced from a whole pig, impregnated with garlic and thyme, turned on a spit as rosy-cheeked children danced around and...

But no matter. The feast was over. Manolo belched and swilled away the last crumbs with wine. The children rolled about the terrace, chasing the dogs and goats, and Manolo's wife went on working. The radio was playing. Manolo looked at me.

"Can you understand that?" he asked.

"Sure, I can hear it."

"Yes, but that's Spanish music and you are not Spanish. How can you understand it?"

It was a question I had never considered. So I looked at Antonio. He grinned and offered to refill Manolo's glass. But at that moment a goat bounded past. Manolo sprang after it and grabbed hold of a hind-leg. He hauled the animal across to me.

"*Hombre*, give me your glass."

He emptied the wine dregs and held the glass under the goat's bulging udder. Fresh warm milk spurted out as Manolo squeezed the animal's teats. Holding out the brimming glass, he flashed his tooth.

"Take it. Nothing better than fresh milk."

There was no way out. I took the glass of warm milk and recalled stories about Malta fever and typhoid and looked at Manolo's expectant grin and downed the rich liquid. It mingled perfectly with the olive oil, vinegar and pork lumps in my stomach. Manolo's hospitality was exceptional, no doubt about it.

I recovered, eventually. But for a long time afterwards a shiver ran down my spine when anybody suggested a nice weekend in the country.

12

WINTER RAINS

You knew when winter had arrived. Women flitted about the village, muttering *"Ay, qué frío! Qué frío!"* while they held scarves over their mouths "to keep out the bad air." At dusk fires flamed on every street. Black figures stooped over the *braseros* (iron bowls filled with blazing sticks), occasionally prodding or blowing. When the fires had died down to red-hot embers, the house-wives took the braziers indoors and set them under the round living-room table.

In the evenings, the whole family sat at the table, spreading a *camilla* (a thick table-cloth) over their knees to contain the rising heat. The mother knitted or crocheted, the children agonised over school-books, the father exchanged gossip while rolling yet another cigarette of pungent, black tobacco, boy and girlfriends flirted with their eyes. All seated facing one another, their legs toasting comfortably below the cloth. It looked about as cosy a scene as you could imagine.

The reality, naturally, was slightly different. The children were fed up with studying. Father was more likely to be away drinking with his mates, or wishing he were. The courting couple, bored out of their minds, were probably plotting how they could snatch a moment alone together, somewhere, sometime. As everybody's backsides turned to ice.

With their thick walls, the village houses were designed to stay cool. They did the job perfectly in mid-summer. In winter, they did it even better. Nasty winds rampaged down from the sierra, jousted with the chimneys, sought out the myriad cracks and openings in window-frames, doors and tiles, then whistled straight through the houses. Insulation and draught-excluders were unknown. But they would have been pointless anyway, because front doors—except when a real storm struck—were always left open. Not only was it unneighbourly to close your door, it was also unnecessary, for nobody appeared to notice the ice-box conditions.

Only feeble strangers bothered with the mess of open fires. This was partly because chimney designs had not made much progress since the time of Pedro the Cruel and they puffed more smoke into the houses than they extracted. Even so, once we had got the pine and olive logs crackling and plugged the worst of the draughts and mulled some wine, at least an illusion of warmth pervaded our house.

On a winter's night, when mist seeped up the valley and muffled sound and sight, the *pueblo* no longer felt Mediterranean. Instead, it became a true mountain community, isolated and turned in on itself. The feeling was redoubled when the rains came, often with tremendous force. Within minutes the streets would be converted into torrents, the steps leading to our house a series of waterfalls.

Rainy days were welcome. Not only did the thought of all that life-giving liquid drenching the soil, *their* soil, bring joy to the hearts of the farmers, but it meant a holiday. They crowded the bars, of which there were an astonishing number. Not that a stranger to the village—nor a government inspector for that matter—could have found most of the bars, for they bore no outward indication. They were often no more than a householder's tiny front room, where even the most miserly could afford to buy drinks all around. As the rain tumbled down, the locals debated the price of fertilizer and sweet potatoes, played dominoes and cards, told tall stories and consumed a certain amount of alcohol. Entering a rainy-day bar was to enter a raucous, intimate world, reeking of thick tobacco smoke, sweat, fried fish, beer and brandy fumes.

One evening, as thunder boomed around the sierras, I visited the neighbouring town for a haircut, not trusting the skills of horny-handed Juanito in the *pueblo*, who ploughed by day and razored by night. As I waited my turn, the storm that had been threatening finally broke, with unusual violence. The drains could not cope with the downpour and the street outside the barber's shop swiftly became a river.

The barber shrugged, laid mats against the door, and showed me to his chair. He clipped merrily away, as the rain continued to thunder down. Soon water began to flow under the door and through the shop. It rose inch by inch. The clients joked and took their shoes off, but the barber kept working. Then the lights failed. At this, he shrugged apologetically.

"That's it. Sorry, but I can do no more," he said. "Come back another time."

So, half-shorn, I paddled through the streets. But there was no chance of reaching home that night. Muddy, debris-strewn water was racing along the usually dry riverbed outside town and swirling about the pillars of the only crossing-point, an old stone bridge. The bridge had sagged dangerously and was impassable. In those days, it only needed one severe storm to cut half the coast off; if the roads were out, telephones and electricity often went, too. The rains had washed away retaining walls, spilling precious soil down the hillsides, ripped up tracks, swamped houses and created the usual havoc. It took 24 hours for me to reach home. For several days I listed to starboard, until I could return to the barber so that he could complete the haircut and restore my balance.

But the rains never lasted long and the sunny days that followed made up for them. There was a brilliance to the atmosphere in winter which I have seen nowhere else. The air possessed an astonishing clarity; every time that I gazed out at the morning stillness from our terrace, I was surprised again by the intensity of the play of light and shadow. Each tree, each house, each ridge, each leaf seemed freshly minted and each image so burnished that it etched itself diamond-sharp on the retina.

The onset of winter was marked by important rituals. On the

night of All Saints' Day, the village came together to keep the souls of their dead relatives company. Families carried bunches of chrysanthemums up the hill to the cemetery, where the departed rested in rank upon rank of sealed chambers in the cemetery walls. Each family owned a niche, where several persons could be interred. To make way for a new corpse, the remains of the old coffin were taken out and burned and the bones pushed to the back. However, as the dead were allowed five years before they could be disturbed, some families also bought a second slot to hold in reserve. Only paupers suffered the ignominy of being buried in the earth and wealthier families preferred to construct mausoleums of marble and alabaster.

On All Saints' Day, the womenfolk meticulously cleaned up the facades of their family tombs, often a precarious task as they had to use ladders to reach the higher rows. Then they arranged the flowers and lit oil-lamps. All night, until the *Día de los Difuntos* (All Souls' Day) dawned, the lights glowed and there was murmured conversation beneath the cypresses in the cemetery, as relatives came and went.

In December came the start of the olive-picking season and the slaughter of pigs for the preparation of hams and sausages in time for the family feast at Christmas. Foreign influences such as Christmas trees and Santa Claus were creeping into the celebration of Christmas, but it was still a religious event rather than an excuse for a Bacchanal. At midnight on Christmas Eve, the church was crowded for Mass and a choir—blessed with more enthusiasm than vocal charm—sang traditional songs. *Los Reyes* (Twelfth Night) remained the traditional occasion for children to receive presents, although televison was working its pernicious influence and children began crying for presents on both dates.

On Christmas Day a procession made its way through the streets. It was a low-key affair, related not to the birth of Christ but to a terrible disaster last century. An earthquake had devastated parts of Málaga and Granada provinces on Christmas Day, 1884, killing thousands. Chroniclers told horrendous stories of houses tumbling into chasms and of people desperately seeking shelter from the winter cold by burying themselves in heaps of steaming manure.

In the *pueblo*, a few houses had tumbled down but nobody had been hurt. The terrified villagers had decamped to a nearby ridge for several days as more tremors shook the province. Earthquakes were not uncommon in the zone and several times I awakened to find my bed rocking violently. The tremors would dislodge large boulders in the sierras and send them tumbling down into the *barrancos*. Such reminders encouraged the village to take out insurance; every year they gave thanks to God for deliverance.

Christmas also brought the thump of *zambombas* and the rustic rhythms of the *Pastores* (shepherds). The *zambomba* was about the most sexually suggestive musical instrument you could imagine, consisting of an earthenware pot with a goatskin stretched across one end. A stick was attached to the skin and the player rubbed his hand up and down the stick with vigorous movements to produce a sound close to a high-decibel fart. Preceded by a diminutive angel and garbed in goat or sheep skins, the shepherds sang carols, but in a way which bore no resemblance to the gentle melodies of "Oh, Come All Ye Faithful" or "Silent Night." To the steady throb of the *zambombas* and the clash of castanets and tambourines, they chanted the words with a hypnotic cadence.

The music is believed to be related to the *fandanguillos* of Huelva and, in turn, to the *jota* of Northern Spain, but it also owes something to the *verdiales*, a primitive, driving style said to have originated with Moorish olive-pickers and which lives on in the Málaga mountains.

Antonio, an open-faced, middle-aged countryman, led the *pastores*, inspiring them with his enthusiasm. He composed the songs and put them to music inside his head while tramping along the mule-tracks or hoeing the fields. "We shouldn't lose these village customs," said Antonio. "They come from the people and help unite them. They are our roots."

El Día de los Reyes (the Day of the Kings) is celebrated with sumptuous processions in many Spanish cities. The *pueblo* festivities held on the evening of January 5 were not quite so elaborate. No camels or elephants or elaborate floats. Just the Three Kings, robes flying, beards slipping, parading through the village and hurling kilos of sweets to the screaming children. They were accompanied by Mary, riding a donkey, with a doll representing the infant Jesus. In later years, sophisticated modern ideas took their toll and she arrived on the back of a truck.

In January, poor old San Sebastian, a quiverful of arrows lodged in his blood-smeared body, was carried from the church and paraded through the streets. When he got back to the *plaza*, he was carefully positioned facing the church so that he could have the best view of the fireworks display that sizzled and swooshed across the white-washed facade.

On bright winter days, families trekked out to their olive groves to collect the ripe fruit. It was a monotonous task, spreading nets below the trees, beating at the branches, then collecting the olives. A few migrant workers from poorer villages in the interior helped with the picking, but generally it was a family affair. The profit margin was so little for these small-scale farmers that they could rarely afford to pay wages.

"Sure, it's slave labour," admitted Juan, a young bachelor. "But I have to keep in my future father-in-law's good books by working on his farm at weekends. One day he's going to leave his land to his children and I want my share then."

The harvest came in by mule and truck to the co-operative, where the presses worked over-time, crushing the olives, and running the juice off into great vats. Each family took 50 or 60 kilos of oil to last the year. It was raw, rich stuff, cloudy, yellow-green, untreated by any heating or chemical process. Virgin olive oil that left a deposit in the *arrobas* (16-litre containers) and would cost a fortune to buy in fancy city delicatessens.

February brought the first strawberries for there were no frosts to sear the young plants here. It also brought *Carnaval,* an excuse to let one's hair down and to invent scandalous verses ridiculing those in authority. Not surprisingly, General Franco banned this *fiesta* as subversive, but after his departure it had staged a big revival. In some towns, groups spent all year preparing their costumes, but in the *pueblo* it was a diversion for youngsters rather than an adult affair.

Often in winter, the peaks behind the *pueblo* would be brushed with snow. Only once or twice in living memory, however, had snow flakes actually drifted down on the village. Planting and harvesting went on year round. At almost any season pairs of heavily muscled cows with blunted horns were toiling along the terraced fields, ploughing the soil for the next crop.

Sometimes the mountain summits could be white as late as April, a reminder that true winter lay just to the north beyond the sierras. But, by the time *Carnaval* came along, the almond trees were already in blossom, the first indication that spring was on the way.

13

CENCERRAZO

Maybe it was the damp winter weather. Maybe it was the last of the wine. Maybe it was time dragging between one *fiesta* and the next. Maybe everybody just needed an excuse. But suddenly the village blew its top. A collective madness gripped the inhabitants. They sang, they danced, they laughed, and they made enough noise to echo through the mountains to Granada and back. Nobody will forget the *cencerrazo*, least of all the centre of the whole crazy affair, *La Gorda* (the Fat One) and her new husband.

The first hint that something unusual was afoot came one evening when a group of children paraded through the cobbled streets. They hauled old cans and sheets of rusty metal behind them and the village rang to the banging and clanging of assorted hardware. Soon others joined the game. A dead bicycle, somebody's plumbing and lengths of chain were added to the collection. The noise volume swelled and swelled until it sounded as though a runaway locomotive was battering its way through a scrap yard.

The village youngsters converged on the home of *La Gorda*, an exuberant, well-upholstered mother of innumerable children whose first husband had died some years earlier. When the news spread that she planned to remarry, village memories had stirred.

"In the old days, when somebody married again, we always had a *cencerrazo*," recalled one old-timer, his face lighting up. "It was a tradition that everybody gathered outside the house and made a heck of a din. And if the couple were bad-tempered about it, then the longer it went on. I remember one lasted 20 days. It might be still going on now if the police hadn't put a stop to it.

"Mind you, the last time the youngsters tried to start a *cencerrazo* it was a bit of an anti-climax. They gathered outside the widow's place, which happened to be right opposite the priest's house. He was a right *aguafiestas* (killjoy). He heard the racket and was very annoyed. He came out, grabbed one of the kids by the ear and told him to clear off. And that was that."

This time, however, the priest was no spoilsport. Paco El Cura appeared to revel in the spirit of the occasion as much as the soon-to-be-weds. Rockets were going off outside their house, drums were beating and the crowd grew as adults joined the throng. The *cencerrazo* (literally meaning "blow of a cowbell") was under way. Joking allusions to the lucky couple crackled around the narrow street. El Colorín, one of the village characters noted for his ability to think up humorous *coplas*, arrived and soon the bystanders were rocking to his scurrilous verses.

The party went on until the small hours. But it had only just begun. The weather co-operated. The following day it rained, and the workers could not go out to the fields. The bars were filled with smoke and reminiscences about what had happened the night before. With every glass of wine, the general euphoria increased and the idea of the *cencerrazo* grew more attractive. The village's imagination had been caught. The couple were due to be married that evening. They must have a memorable send-off.

And that meant noise, noise at a decibel level that made the previous evening's cacophony seem like the hush at a librarian's funeral. Young men dashed along the streets, towing a bath that smashed against the cobbles with deafening force. A derelict stove, pieces of corrugated iron, oil drums entered the fray. The whole valley reverberated. The village forgot about television and peered down from balconies and rooftops to watch the fun.

Bizarre-looking couples were making their appearance in the narrow streets to the delight of the onlookers. Giggles followed the

progress of a young man with an eyepatch and a suitcase as he guided his blushing bride down the street. The spoof bride clutched a baby doll to her bosom with tender bricklayers' hands. Other ladies in flowery headgear and with extraordinary physical development minced past.

"This is better than the *feria*," yelled one villager.

Indeed, the village had erupted into a carnival, an uninhibited release of energy. The *cencerrazo* is said to have pagan roots. Perhaps originally all the noise was intended to drive out evil spirits. Then it became a way to register a moral protest, a way to shame any spouse for affronting local custom by remarrying. More educated Spaniards tended to be contemptuous of such manifestations of public emotion, regarding them as examples of medieval backwardness. The authorities viewed them with disfavour too, no doubt fearing that the whole business could get out of hand and constitute a threat to law and order. I noticed that the mayor and the dignitaries of our community, as well as the municipal policemen, were nowhere in evidence.

But almost everybody else seemed to have no inhibitions whatever. Outside *La Gorda's* house the crowd was jammed wall to wall. The crowd flowed down the hill to the church square where a posse of oddly-attired individuals commandeered a jeep. Just as an attempt was made to drive the vehicle away, its chassis almost touching the ground, two heads in patent-leather tricorn hats bobbed into view amid the crowd. The Civil Guards had arrived on the scene.

They and their families kept apart from the village, living in a decaying barracks. In the bitter years after the Civil War there had been a large detachment stationed there, but now there were only four or five. They were still feared, for they represented the authority of Madrid. They patrolled the rural byways and kept note of everything that passed in the *pueblo* and it did not pay to run afoul of them.

The sergeant surveyed the chaotic scene in the plaza in horror. But he could see that things had reached a pitch where tactful handling was required. He kept his voice calm as he suggested that the passengers should dismount from the jeep. Then he headed for the centre of activity, *La Gorda's* house.

There the racket had reached a crescendo with the arrival of the priest who was to carry out the wedding service in the bride's living room. The bridegroom must have wondered as he gazed out at the milling crowds whether he had bitten off more than he could chew. The Civil Guards made half-hearted efforts to cool things down. The sergeant remonstrated with a man beating a large oil drum.

"That's enough! This disturbance has gone on long enough," he declared.

He might as well have tried to halt a tidal wave. The drum-beating continued. *El Chico*, looking even more diabolical than usual, was capering about, encouraging the crowd with frantic gesticulations. A wild-eyed youth was repeatedly lifting a bath above his head and dashing it down on the cobbles, picking it up and smashing it down again. Another was doing a crazy dance with a lighted candle planted on his head. Another was beating an old bicycle to pieces, roaring with delight.

"Didn't you hear me? I said that's enough," cried the sergeant. He was unused to disobedience. These were the days of the Franco regime when nobody dared challenge a Civil Guard.

A murmur went up from the crowd, gathering courage from their numbers, forgetting their fears and taboos in the excitement of the moment.

"Out! Out!" they chanted.

El Chico roared his approval. He cackled excitedly and made obscene gestures.

"Out! Out!" he cried, too.

The sergeant's face flushed with anger. You could guess the thoughts flashing through his head. This was outrageous, unheard-of. By God, it was open defiance, anarchy, mutiny.

"Out! Out!"

The chant grew louder. The villagers no longer cared about the possible repercussions. Their pent-up rebelliousness erupted. Nobody was going to spoil their fun. The sergeant's hand hovered near the revolver at his waist. Suddenly the situation threatened to turn ugly. One wrong move and anything could happen. The threat of mob violence was in the air. It only needed the spark, it only needed the Civil Guard to pull that gun.

Suddenly, a deluge of water hurled from a rooftop sloshed over part of the crowd. The sergeant narrowly missed being soaked. He glared around at the exalted faces and hesitated.

"Out! Out!" cried the people.

How does anybody handle a *cencerrazo*? With kid gloves. The Civil Guards exchanged glances and decided that discretion was called for. They melted away, good humour held sway, and the party went on.

A cheer went up. The bride and groom had appeared. The Fat One revelled in this rare moment of public attention. She smiled and waved in regal style. Her beau, a widower as lean as she was amply proportioned, looked ready to take to the hills. Arm in arm, they were swept down the precipitous street to the plaza where Manolo was waiting with his taxi. Smiling bravely, they took their seats but the vehicle could not move. Manolo got out and pleaded for room. The crowd moved back a few inches, but refused to allow the couple to leave the square by the main exit. Instead, the taxi had to traverse the entire length of the main street, bounced constantly on its springs and attended by a dancing, singing escort.

The journey to the edge of the village took more than an hour. Even then, the bride and her groom were lucky to escape, for the mob fully intended to accompany them to the next town. Only some fast manoeuvring by Manolo finally extricated them. Growing desperate at the footmarks over his precious vehicle, he saw an opening, gunned the accelerator and the taxi shot away over the brow of the hill, the happy couple waving furiously from the rear window.

The villagers floated home on a cloud of euphoria. The banging and the crashing were stilled. The *cencerrazo* was over. Finally, the *pueblo* could sleep.

14

THE VISITORS

Friends of friends, they sat in our living room inspecting the whitewash and sipping a pricey Rioja.

"Not bad, this Spanish plonk," he said, "Of course, at home we usually stick to Bordeaux. Yes, those Frenchies know a thing or two about making wine."

In the kitchen I corked the vintage Rioja and refilled their glasses with an evil concoction generously donated by previous guests.

She was admiring the view when I returned.

"Beautiful! And I do envy you this lovely sunshine. Do you spend much time here?"

"All year."

"Really. I can see it's a fantastic place for a holiday, so restful, but it is a bit...er...out of the way. I mean, how do you fill your days?"

"Oh, drinking wine and thinking about mañana," I replied, inwardly cursing at the time being frittered away while a pile of work awaited attention.

He chuckled.

"Fantastic! What a life! I envy you." He savoured the contents of his glass and tossed back the wine. "You know, I could get a taste for this. Get home often?"

"Actually, this is our home."

Somehow it came out like an apology. They glanced around at the two threadbare armchairs a penniless remittance man had given us in exchange for an airline ticket to Gatwick, at the table made by the local carpenter and at the esparto mat woven by an old muleteer.

"Rather knuckles-on-the-ground territory, isn't it? I mean, a trifle primitive?"

"We get on fine. The locals are very friendly."

"Speak the lingo, too? My, my. But how long do you expect to stay?"

"Indefinitely."

His eyebrows lifted.

"But, I mean, eventually, I mean... " He seemed embarrassed at having to spell it out. "Well, you will be going home, back to the Old Country?"

"I very much doubt it. Frankly, I prefer it here."

He raised his eyebrows and a sudden chill killed off further conversation. Soon afterwards, they tottered off down the hill, eager to escape the traitors' nest. They were speeded on their way down the street by El Chico. His fiendish chuckles and leering gestures no longer alarmed us, but they produced dramatic reactions in our departing guests.

My wife restored her spirits with the Rioja.

"I don't think I need any more visitors." she said.

It wasn't like that at the start. In our early days we were brimming with hospitality, eager to show off the delights of *pueblo* living. We soon found there were plenty ready to share our experience. And our house. And our food. They turned up unannounced and stayed for a week or a month, impervious to hints about moving on, deaf to insults. Friends were all right. It was the total strangers, friends of friends and the friends of friends of friends, who put the tin hat on it. Even the least subtle of hints made no impression on them.

Thea found Jerry, an easygoing Aussie with a vague recommendation from Down Under, on the doorstep one winter's evening. She invited him in for a moment and he stayed two weeks. He made little conversation, except with a whisky bottle, settling in front of our fire as though he was waiting for spring. His arrival stirred the neighbours' imaginations for it coincided with my absence on a working trip. Gifted with a sixth sense, he decamped just before my return, leaving Thea with no firewood, a pile of empty bottles and a reputation she wasn't looking for.

However, Jerry was easy to take compared to Rosie and her infant daughter. They were waiting on the doorstep one day when I toiled up the street. They were on their way back home to New York but Rosie was in no hurry to get there.

"Hi, I'm a friend of Dean and he said it would be okay to stay here."

"Dean?"

"He's a chum of Sidney's."

"Sorry, who's Sidney?"

"He's a buddy of Phil."

Finally a name I recognised. Phil, an old friend, was due any moment. I did the decent thing and gave Rosie a bed for the night. It was a fatal mistake. The next day Phil, his wife and three small children arrived. He had never heard of Rosie, but she regarded his arrival as a guarantee that she and her baby could stay, indefinitely.

Soon there came another knock at the door. It was my brother, eager to see our *pueblo* house. We squeezed him in. A day or so later, Colin turned up. I vaguely remembered inviting him along during a beery night in a Shropshire pub and he had taken me at my word. We squeezed him in, too. Full of the initial infatuation with our new life, we welcomed everybody in. The neighbours watched events with increasing interest.

Sleeping arrangements for seven adults and four children in a one-and-a-half-bedroom house were somewhat complex. Privacy was minimal. The old beams rattled and creaked under the stress of so many under one roof. Although apparently bereft of funds, Rosie acted the lady of leisure while her daughter Janie demonstrated her abilities as a three-year-old terrorist. She had swift, grasping hands and lungs of daunting power. She dominated the house with her extravagant demands. Some were more extravagant than others.

"I wanna Jumbo!" she would bellow. "I wanna Jumbo!"

"That's my Janie," cooed her mother. "She wants to fly Jumbo jet."

Conversation in jetsetter Janie's presence was impossible. When the other children had gone to bed, she was still among us, throwing tantrums and food about. She was in training for New York.

There was not enough space around the dining table for all, nor much on it, as we were all short of funds and Rosie showed no inclination to pay her share. But that situation was soon alleviated. Stomach upsets reduced the numbers at mealtimes to manageable proportions. Half our residents were groaning on their beds at any one time. A constant succession of ashen-faced adults and infants hurried into the street and in via the stable door to the downstairs toilet, while the neighbours shook their heads in amazement at the busy traffic.

Relations with our nearest and dearest neighbour were not improved by a minor incident involving the children. They had set up a rubber paddling pool on the terrace and were happily playing there, when suddenly Pura came flying through the front door. Her face had lost all vestige of its usual patient serenity. It was as black as her dress. She stormed through the house and on to the terrace and confronted the children. They shrank back fearfully.

"Is she a witch?" they asked.

Pura could have been forgiven for casting a spell over them. She had been working in her kitchen, she explained, when a nasty-smelling liquid had cascaded down the ventilation shaft straight into her stew bubbling away on the stove. The children confessed that they had poured the contents of a plastic chamber pot down a handy vent on the terrace. Abject apologies and expressions of sympathy were necessary to cool the situation.

When it seemed things could only get better, a bout of malaria struck down Colin and he took to his camp bed, which happened to be in the living room as there was nowhere else to put it. There he lay sweating and shivering under blankets as the children played hide and seek around him. Callers nervously inquired about the odd bundle in the corner and it required considerable fortitude to ignore his pitiful quaking figure, as we tucked into our rich diet of sardines and garbanzos.

After several weeks even rhino-skinned Rosie gathered that she was out-staying her welcome. She prepared to move out and we prepared to celebrate with champagne. But the night before her departure, Janie tumbled head first down the bedroom steps. She awoke the entire village with her cries as blood poured from a gash under one eye.

At the doctor's I found myself playing the role of father, helping to hold down the fighting, screaming child while a stitch was inserted. The doctor glanced at me in a way that made plain what he thought of my paternal abilities.

"She's not mine!" I wanted to shout. "She's not mine!"

Worse was to come. Rosie, playing on the situation, forgot all about moving out and stayed another week.

That experience should have been lesson enough, but we dismissed Rosie as an aberration. Other visitors came. One couple, bored with one another, were clearly looking for adventure, nudge, nudge.

"Do you mind if I kiss your husband?" the wife inquired of Thea. "I've never kissed a man with a beard."

"And I've never kicked anybody," said the expression on Thea's face.

They were interested in games that only four could play and the best defence we could think of was to pretend to an innocence that would have done credit to Red Riding Hood.

The last straw came when a leftwing activist from London arrived with her brood and boyfriend. Considering her political views, she showed an oddly aristocratic reluctance to lift a finger with the chores. Below stairs, Thea's days were filled with shopping, cooking and washing up. Soon explosion point was reached. Giving up our bed was one thing, being treated as part of Room Service was another. We decided to beat a tactical retreat and leave the whole place to the family for the rest of their holiday while we headed for Granada on suddenly important business.

It was a relief to escape, but soon serious doubts began to nag us. Our guest had made a name for herself on her home patch as a militant squatters' leader. Suppose she invited her friends over. Suppose that in our absence our home was invaded by refugees from London's East End, out-of-work dockers and tattooed soccer hooligans, big, beefy, pugnacious types, all prepared to stay forever.

On our return we struggled warily up the street. But there were no punks hanging out of the windows, no graffiti on the walls, no scrawled messages warning "Skinheads rule, okay". The house was intact, more or less, and quite empty.

We sat on our terrace and looked down the valley towards the sea. In our absence the swifts had arrived, shrilling over the *pueblo* in spectacular aerobatics. Our peach tree was in blossom and fresh greenery clothed the hills.

Spring was here. And the visitors had gone.

15

POLITICS HIT THE PUEBLO

You could not go into one of the local bars without hearing about it. There was going to be an election, a proper one with political parties. You could vote for any one, even the Communists. It was the first time in 40 years that Spain had held free democratic elections. General Franco had dispensed with such nonsense, which in his view only confused the people. His regime had seemed destined to go on forever. Now, suddenly, he was gone and everybody had to adjust to a new system.

Faustino, the mayor, was the first to show his political flexibility. Like all mayors, he had not been elected but appointed to the post with Madrid's approval. On the whole he had done a good job, introducing a number of enlightened measures, including building controls to preserve the *pueblo*'s traditional style of architecture. But his authoritarian style had rubbed some people up the wrong way.

"He tried to ban us from riding our mules along the main street. He tried to stop us singing in the bars. And he had the nerve to name a street after himself," they complained.

Changing times, however, had had a remarkably liberalising effect on Franco's appointee. Suddenly all the talk was of socialism and he was not going to miss out.

"Myself," he proclaimed in the bar one evening, "I'm a socialist at heart—but a moderate."

Benito, the new *practicante*, bearded and overflowing with missionary fervour, scoffed at this: "How can you be a socialist with your record? Nobody here knows what socialism is all about. They have to be educated."

All this was too much for Melchor, an aged peasant with cross eyes and sagging trousers. He banged his drink on the counter and elbowed into the conversation.

"Nonsense!" rasped Melchor, whose vocal chords had been sandpapered by a lifetime's addiction to alcohol and black tobacco. "I'm the only true socialist among the lot of you. I like being sociable and I enjoy social activities. What I say is 'Viva José Antonio!' "

Nobody was unkind enough to point out that José Antonio could hardly be classed as a socialist, especially as he founded the Falange (Spain's fascist party).

It was not surprising that the *pueblo* was confused, for political parties had been banned since the end of the Civil War. Hardly anybody could remember the previous elections, held before the war. For four decades the National Movement had controlled every phase of life. Political debate was stifled. Newspapers—if they wanted to keep publishing—mirrored a stable, Catholic Spain and an outside world riddled with Communist-Masonic subversion, pornography and corruption. The Caudillo ruled like a stern father.

As Don Calixto pointed out: "He must be popular with the people. When they held a national referendum, he got 98 per cent of the vote."

Don Calixto had his finger on the pulse because he had been one of Franco's mayors. His reign had been mercifully brief, but he had established a certain popularity, particularly among those who stayed the pace with him as he drank the night away, cracking ribald jokes. His mandate had become legendary for its displays of fascist fervour. About 3am he liked to marshall his fellow-drinkers outside the bar and march them through the village streets, barking out commands.

"*Oiga*, Pepe, you must be a Red—you're out of step with everybody," he would bellow, to alcoholic chortles. Bringing his staggering squad to a halt outside the Civil Guard headquarters, he would address a few rousing words to them, then raise his right arm in salute and lead them in a discordant rendering of the Falangist anthem, *Cara al Sol*. As dawn broke, Calixto would crawl up to the schoolhouse where, through his hangovers, he endeavoured to teach the village youngsters how to be clean-living Spaniards.

Even with such fervent supporters as Don Calixto, General Franco had lost his grip towards the end. His Christmas television broadcasts revealed him as a shaky, puppet-like figure, with a quavering voice. All the Franco jokes that had once been recounted in whispers for fear of a swift journey to the lockup began to be heard openly.

"Did you hear about Franco on his deathbed?" asked Benito. "The word gets around, see, that he is not long for this world and thousands of people begin gathering outside El Pardo palace. He hears the noise and asks his wife 'Carmen, what's happening? What do the people want?' So Doña Carmen replies 'Francisco, they have come to say goodbye.'

"And Franco says 'Goodbye? But where are they going?' "

When El Caudillo finally did say goodbye, after agonizing weeks in hospital, his passing came with a whimper rather than a bang. One morning we woke up and the momentous news was out. I looked out of the window but there was nobody dancing in the street. The Reds had not emerged from under their beds to proclaim a revolution. The *ultras*, the rightwingers, were not parading up and down in their blue shirts. The truth was that nobody could really believe the implacable little general had gone.

People were fearful about what the future held. For 40 years it had all been so clear-cut. The remote father figure had decided everything, and only heroes or fools had dared oppose him. Either you were for Franco, or you were against, in which case you kept your mouth shut. Now there was a dangerous void.

A few days later a welcome rainstorm drenched the fields and Alcachofa nodded sagely.

"It's Franco," she said. "He has gone to heaven and told them we need rain. Even in death he is working for us."

Pretty soon, a new government began dismantling Franco's system. The benefits of democracy were soon apparent. They began selling pornography on the news stalls and banned films like Deep Throat, Emmanuelle and Lusty Virgins hit the cinemas. *Destape* (striptease) became the in-word. Everywhere you looked in Spain there was *destape*, either *destape* in the flesh or metaphorical *destape*—*flamenco con destape, circo con destape, destape del escándalo político.*

Finally, the echoes reached as far as the *pueblo*.

Rafael, a bricklayer, welcomed the changes with open arms, arms like girders after years working in construction.

"Democracy." He rolled the new word around his mouth, savouring it like a chunk of sausage. "Democracy is what we want. So that everybody has a fair chance and can live in proper style. All those big villas with swimming pools we've been building on the coast for rich foreigners, they belong to the Spanish people. They're on our soil, built with our sweat. We're going to turf out the foreigners and live there ourselves. After the elections, of course, or it wouldn't be democratic."

Considering the new-found interest in politics, the village was a little disappointed when the general election campaign began. No fewer than 153 of the 156 parties taking part somehow overlooked our existence. People were too proud to show that they were hurt, wondering whether it was the narrow mountain road or the lethal effects of our *vino del terreno* that deterred the candidates. Even so, the *pueblo* was pained that Felipe González, the young Socialist Party leader whose tousled, tieless image showed he was a man of the people, could zip from one end of the country to the other by executive jet, but could not spare the time for the mule-trip up to the *pueblo*. Worse, his lot never even put up a poster.

The three parties that did show up were sadly uninformed on local priorities. Their representatives pontificated earnestly about the need for a new constitution, about human rights, about the perils of communism and the need to bury the past. But the Great Papas Disaster barely got a mention. That was the big issue and they acted as though it had never happened. When the price of papas (as potatoes were popularly known) slumped to seven pesetas a kilo that spring, virtually the whole *pueblo* went into mourning.

"Look at this beauty," said my neighbour Miguel, showing me a potato the size of a melon. "Months of work growing it and now it's not worth digging up!"

The speaker from the Andalusian Party, a young fellow in a beard and a sports shirt, had an answer.

"Form co-operatives to fight for your rights—then you'll get better prices," he advised.

He was a university professor, obviously sincere, obviously eager for change. But how many papas had he grown? How had the rising price of fertilizer affected him? The villagers, each with his tiny plot of land won from the mountainside and tended with infinite care, were sceptical.

"You say you'll break up the big estates," said one, "Does that mean we can take over those great vineyards in Jerez?"

Patiently, the professor explained that things must be done legally, step by step. First there would have to be constitutional changes.

"Then we won't be picking those grapes tomorrow?" said the villager, with such obvious disappointment that everyone burst into laughter.

Meetings were held in the cinema, dimly enough lit so that you hardly noticed the walls stained by damp. Most of the audience sat in the 10-peseta stalls, but discreeter souls kept to the 15-peseta balcony. Now and again people would glance over their shoulders rather nervously, still unconvinced that the wrath of the law was not about to descend on them. As long as most of them could remember, attending such an assembly would have been enough to guarantee a speedy trip to jail. Perhaps that's why there was no heckling and few were brave enough to ask embarrassing questions.

When the ogres of 40 years arrived, people were dumb-founded. Could that really be a picture of Karl Marx up there, flanked by two mighty hammers and sickles? Why hadn't the Civil Guard stopped the meeting and arrested everybody involved in it? Even more confusing were the words of the Communist candidate, a hefty, shirt-sleeved farm worker, who made no call to arms to oust the capitalist oppressors and never mentioned "revolution." Instead, he declared his support for democracy and asked for donations as Moscow was not sending any gold.

The man from the Centrists, an opportunist coalition hastily cobbled together by Prime Minister Adolfo Suárez, looked more like a bank manager than a son of the soil, but he also supported democracy. He was impeccable in a city suit. Many of his listeners wore suits and ties, too, and their wives were immaculately turned out for the occasion. He said comforting things about stability and responsibility and how experience counted (an oblique reference to his term in Franco's government) and they applauded frequently. Things promised to liven up when subversive elements asked why 18-year-olds could not vote and why the candidate had recently changed his political colours after serving the Generalísimo so faithfully. The meeting ended unusually quickly, before anyone could get on to the subject of papas.

Political debate did not exactly reach fever pitch on the Street of Bitterness. Alcachofa said she wasn't going to any of those meetings: "my husband would beat me." Pura, in her 80s, recalled the violence of the past and trembled at what political change might bring. "I just hope there's no trouble like last time, before the war. I remember the Rojos smashing all the statues in the church. They used Christ's head as a football, they did. And then came the Nationalists and shot them all."

This time, however, passions appeared surprisingly muted. On polling day, Placido forsook his work as rates collector, traffic warden, farmer, and savings bank agent. He put on his municipal policeman's uniform and guarded democracy outside the local school. Two Civil Guards were on duty too, fingering their sub-machine guns uncertainly. Nobody was quite sure whose side they were on.

Everyone queued peacefully, enjoying the novelty of casting a vote. When the results were in, they showed that Felipe González had made a profound tactical error. Since he had snubbed the *pueblo*, it had responded in kind and ignored him and his party. The feared Rojos had done even worse—the villagers had long memories. The professor's Andalusian party gained a respectable vote, but most of the villagers put their cross against the name of the man with the natty suit. Fast footwork had won him a seat in Madrid again.

The old guard was clinging on to power. Even so, there was definitely a new feeling around.

"Wait until the municipal elections. I think I may stand for mayor," said José, a university student. "It's time to change things here and let the youngsters have a say. Why, we haven't even got a football pitch."

Colorín, the breadman who sang satirical coplas, said he might stand, too. Paco, the radical and energetic priest, offered his house for meetings of farmworkers wanting to form a co-operative.

For the first time some in the *pueblo* seemed to think they had a right to criticise and ask awkward questions. If the man in the suit came visiting his constituents, it was clear he had better have a good story prepared about those papas. Could this be what democracy was all about?

16

THE OUTING

It was a tempting enough offer. A trip to the Seville feria at a rockbottom price. Half the *pueblo* was going. Twenty-four hours of revelry guaranteed. An offer you could not refuse. It cost me no heart-searching at all to turn it down.

I did not join the Ceuta excursion either. Nor the one to Tivoli. Nor the outing to Granada and the Sierra Nevada. Nor the Cádiz binge. No way. I have been on a *pueblo* outing and have no need to repeat the experience.

The all-singing, all-action Technicolor Córdoba extravaganza, or more precisely Caridad's outing, was enough. My neighbour had crashed through the front door with her usual easy grace and civility, crying: "*Cojones!* What an opportunity! There's a bus trip to Córdoba on Saturday and so cheap. You can't miss a chance like this."

I had never had any intention of going to Córdoba. It was time to plant a new crop of stones and weeds in the wilderness behind the house. The plumber was due any moment to fix the water heater—he had promised only two months before. The wine festering away in the cellar was due for decanting. This was no time to go gallivanting around the country. I made it plain that Córdoba was out of the question.

The bus left at 4am. Everybody was on it, except Caridad. The minutes ticked by and Antonio revved the engine and peered down the darkened village street, muttering into his stubbly jowls. Somebody was dispatched to find the missing passenger. Finally, shortly before 5 o'clock, Caridad hove into view, bucketing down the street in a whirl-wind of flustered gesticulations, flying hats, skirts and baskets, trailed by what looked like a chorus of scurrying chickens but proved to be her innumerable children. Immaculately coiffed, elaborately made-up, Caridad settled her brood in a front seat and with regal condescension ignored the critical remarks directed at her.

We rumbled off, swinging around hairpin bends, frightening owls and sleeping pigeons, lurching past *cortijos* where mules blinked at us in surprise, down to the coast road. Caridad kept up a lightning dialogue with Bruno the butcher, each shouting at the tops of their voices since they were at opposite ends of the bus. Their obscene allusions and subtle quips kept everybody in convulsions. Or more correctly, it kept Caridad and Bruno in convulsions. The rest of us tried to get some sleep before dawn broke.

Soon we came up behind a heavy truck struggling up a steep incline at walking pace. When we reached a level section, the truck increased speed and hogged the middle of the road. Then came more bends. After trying unsuccessfully for 15 minutes to overtake it, Antonio took his hands off the wheel and waved them about, uttering bus-driver oaths and appealing to the Virgin hanging above his seat. Everybody peered through the windows to study the infidel blocking our path.

"It's Baldomero! It must be. Even here we can't escape him," cried Bruno.

More convulsions. Baldomero drove Spain's oldest and slowest vehicle. No matter what hour of the day or night you approached the *pueblo*, Baldomero always seemed to be ahead of you, struggling along at an agonisingly slow pace and holding up all the traffic. Always so grossly overloaded that it looked ready to split asunder, his lorry never travelled at more than 5 miles per hour and was only met driving uphill. It had never been seen travelling downhill, perhaps because it then moved so fast it was invisible to the human eye.

Eventually we swept past the truck. If it was not Baldomero, it was certainly his twin. There were cheers, jeers and rude gestures from the exalted trippers. After an hour or so, a 10-minute halt was made for coffee, *anís*, cognac, *sol y sombras*, sticky pastries, potato crisps, sunflower seeds and peanuts. An hour later—after an emergency in the cafeteria toilets involving Caridad's children—we were on the road again. The radio was turned up full blast to make everybody feel at home and to give Caridad's voice some competition. As Antonio stepped on the gas to swing past lumbering Baldomeros and other obstacles, the faces of several passengers underwent alarming changes.

The well-built lady next to me groped for a plastic bag as her complexion took on the hues of a badly adjusted colour television screen. The cry went up for "Air! Air!" and windows were hastily flung open before the coffee, *anís*, cognac, lemonade, sticky pastries, potato crisps, sunflower seeds and peanuts made an unwelcome second appearance.

On the outskirts of Córdoba, Caridad leaned across to the driver and, fluttering her eyelids, said: "Listen, can you drop me off before you get to the centre so I can visit my family? It will only take a minute."

Obligingly, Antonio pulled off the main road and entered a side street.

"Straight ahead," commanded Caridad, "Right at the top of the hill, then left at the traffic lights. Now left, then left again. Down that side-street."

Her fellow-passengers looked at each other with a bemused air as we plunged ever deeper into a maze of back streets. Finally, the bus stopped before a small house and Caridad descended. We waited, and waited. The passengers became restive. Then Caridad returned and called to everybody to come and meet her relatives. She darted quickly away before anybody could nail her to her seat. People from the neighbourhood began to gather and gossip. Caridad's children started playing games with the local kids. As the minutes ticked by, Antonio the driver looked at his watch and muttered away.

Caridad popped her head briefly out of a house down the street to say her father had gone for his morning stroll but would be

back soon. We waited, but he failed to return. At length, Caridad had to be forcibly reloaded onto the bus with her children. The bus set off. But a hundred yards down the street she uttered a shriek.

"There he is! There he is!"

Out leaped Caridad to embrace her father. Her children and half the bus followed. Antonio sighed. One or two unsociable types mumbled something about hoping to see the Mosque before sundown.

Their discontent became sharper when it emerged that most of us had not considered coming on the excursion until we had been nobbled by Caridad. Apparently tickets had been selling badly and the whole venture had been about to be called off. That was when Caridad, seeing an opportunity to visit her family fading fast, had launched her private promotion campaign and bullied us all aboard.

"*Vámonos! Vámonos!*" cried my fellow-trippers, starting to lose their patience.

At length, when it looked as though the *pueblo* outing was about to dissolve into a protest demonstration and visions of sirens wailing and visored riot cops began to swim through the imagination, the family reunion broke up. Caridad and her father were bundled on to the bus and we arrived at last in the centre of Córdoba.

A new difficulty then arose. Since Antonio was working to what may be kindly described as a flexible schedule, the party could not split up and meet again at an appointed time for the return journey. For the sake of smooth organisation, we had to stick together. And worse still, due to unforeseen circumstances—Caridad did not bat an eyelid—only half an hour could be allowed to visit the Grand Mosque.

Thirty minutes to appreciate the grandeur of one of the Moors' finest pieces of architecture, 30 minutes to admire this wondrous creation of the caliphs, 30 minutes to examine those 850 columns of jasper and marble, to study the delicate mosaics, to gaze in awe at friezes and cupolas and galleries and Arabesques. We did it. We raced up and down the vast echoing naves. We flashed past chapels and arches, throwing brief, all-embracing glances at the wonders of the past. We scorched past slow-moving groups from Idaho and Munchen-Gladbach, trampled down stray old ladies studying their guidebooks without due care and attention, and with a final burst of speed burst once more into the open.

It was a magnificent operation, carried through with split-second timing. Flushed with triumph, we managed a second-wind sprint to the bus. There was nobody there. Not Antonio. Not Bruno. Not Caridad. Nor anybody else. Just three or four of us, the front-runners. After waiting half an hour during which a few stragglers turned up we decided to drift off and take a look at the bullfight museum. That proved a mistake because in our absence the other half of the party turned up and decided they might as well go and look at the Roman bridge. Since there was still nobody around on our return, we thought we might as well walk over to the Alcázar, thus missing the Roman bridge enthusiasts who, since there was still nobody around, decided that they might as well see what was happening in the Museo Arqueológico.

By the time everybody had been rounded up, it was lunch time. That put the party in good humour, ready for the visit to the zoo. The wildest thing that most of the *pueblo* had seen before was Pepe El Panadero dancing on the Casino bar-top at 3am during the last *fiesta*. Thus the sight of so many bizarre creatures of the wild was an instant source of shock and delight. The zoo was a hit, the hit of the whole outing. Compared to leopards and buffalo and elephants, the boring old Mosque rated zero in the popularity poll. As for the Museo Arqueológico…

The hippopotamus pen drew cries of amazement as its occupants cooled themselves in a pool and yawned in expansive hippo style. Gazing into the abysses thus exposed, Bruno chuckled: "*Ay que ve*! And we thought you had a mouth, Caridad. Look at that one!"

"It looks just like Manolo de los Cuatro Vientos," said another.

"No, it's got more teeth than Manolo."

"Just imagine having to feed him with *papas fritas* every day. It would take the whole potato crop."

Glowing with the cleverness of their wit and the effects of the lunch-time wine, the party moved on to the lions. As Fernando of the tobacco shop edged closer to gape at the beasts, a lion turned his head towards him and let out a mighty roar. Fernando leaped backwards, almost swallowing his cigarette.

"*Por Dios*, Fernando! You're so ugly even the lions can't stand you," yelled one of his friends. Everybody laughed, except Fernando.

Next stop was the monkey house and no sooner did the party catch sight of the chattering, red-bummed animals than they fell about laughing.

"Imagine having to share your bed with one of those Butano-coloured backsides," said Bruno.

"Never mind the backside. What about the front?" cried Caridad, provoking loud guffaws. Except from one or two señoras who eyed Caridad with profound disapproval.

Suddenly there was a disruption. One of the children came running up, his eyes almost popping out of his head.

"Over here, over here!" he shouted, "Come on. You've never seen anything like it."

Everybody lost interest in the monkeys and rushed over to a nearby compound. Their astonishment was unbounded, limitless. They hardly knew whether to laugh or cry. It was just too much.

"*Cojones*! How long do you reckon it is, Paco?"

"Fifty centimetres, I'd say."

"Nah, it's close to a metre, at least."

"We could do with one of them in the *pueblo*," said Caridad.

"You wouldn't get any more complaints from the women."

They kept up the wisecracks for half an hour as they surveyed a zebra on heat and tried to estimate his impressive vital statistics. It was generally agreed that now they had seen it all. None of Córdoba's other diversions were likely to match this.

We had done the city. It was time to go. We climbed back in the bus and headed out of Córdoba. But first we had to drop off Caridad's father. Once again we halted while the old man embraced all the children and kissed Caridad, then embraced the children again, and a few other relatives entered into the spirit of the occasion. A clamour arose from the bus as the ceremony dragged on. Enraged by our lack of compassion, Caridad stormed aboard, eyes flashing, tears streaming down her cheeks.

"Can't I even say goodbye to my own father? Don't you have any feeling? How would you like it if it were your father? I see him only once a year. My own father!"

The children began to cry and the old man standing at the curb put a handkerchief to his eyes. Then the other women on the bus also began to weep. Because it was true. They couldn't stand Caridad. But after all it was her father and they had fathers, too, and it was hard having to say goodbye to your own flesh and blood. Bathed in tears, we lurched out of Córdoba.

But soon the sorrow of parting was forgotten. The radio was turned up full volume, the air was filled with tobacco smoke, and the events of the day were debated. Those who had missed the zebra's performance cursed their luck while the rest chuckled over a steady stream of obscene jokes that ricocheted around the bus. Wild estimates were offered on the size of the hippo's jaws and on other anatomical parts on view at the zoo. We swept across the plain and up mountain passes and Pepe led the singing and the handclapping and somebody passed around a bottle of brandy, until the brain felt like a football bouncing down the highway.

Only on the last stretch up to the *pueblo* did the bus fall silent. It was well after midnight when we rolled to a halt and everybody tumbled out, drained by the rich experiences of the day. Giant hippos and over-endowed zebras haunted the *pueblo* that night and for quite a while afterwards. The Córdoba outing was a fantastic success. That's what Caridad tells me anyhow.

17

THE GODMOTHER

Smugness fitted Dooley the way whitewash suits a *pueblo* house. It was a part of him, like the perfect teeth and the permanently bronzed skin. With his snappy clothes, clipped East Coast accent and knife-edge creases, he could have been a Scott Fitzgerald character about to play host to a Long Island garden party or a Wall Street broker en route to his exclusive tennis club. By some inexplicable mischance, however—the wrong flight connection, perhaps—he ended up in the *pueblo*.

One or two mules blinked at his coming, there were mutterings about "the lost tycoon", but generally his reception was under-whelming. He did his best, wheeling out a succession of anecdotes about his most intimate friends, all apparently rich and famous. But these did not generate much enthusiasm among folk whose conversation tended to dwell on more vital questions like Real Madrid's last game and the chances of winning the lottery.

Not that Dooley was deterred. Soon he became a specialist in "village secrets." Once he unearthed these gems, they magically became his property. Thus the old lady who for years had been selling me her thyme-scented honey was suddenly "discovered" and transformed into "my Maria." Fernando, who had been weaving *esparto* baskets for half a century, became "my weaver." When he came across a cluster of abandoned buildings up in the sierras, Dooley revealed that he had discovered a "lost village." As a favour he passed on the location of "my own little swimming hole," a heavily-frequented reservoir down in the valley. Dooley was a very irritating person.

Even so, he did not deserve The Godmother. Nobody deserved The Godmother. His smugness was his undoing. He was positively purring when he encountered me one day in the street.

"Listen, I've found the perfect woman. You won't believe it. Considerate, intelligent, industrious. She's got it all. Gee, you just don't get around and talk to people or you might have got there first."

Danger signals started flashing. Dooley was so elated it was disturbing. How could I have missed this vision of perfection?

"This woman is fantastic. She cooks like a Cordon Bleu chef. This morning she insisted on re-ironing my clothes—she has so much pride she just could not bear to see me anything but immaculately dressed in public. She is so kindly, too. Today she brought me a bouquet of flowers, yesterday it was a basket of oranges."

"A basket of oranges! Wow!"

"Yep, she's full of olde worlde courtesy. And intelligent. I tell you this woman has a brain."

"Well, that's fantastic," I agreed, "But you haven't mentioned what she looks like. Dark, passionate? Eyes like liquid pools of fire? Built like...like..."

"Like a tank," said Dooley. "Solid, strong, dependable."

"A tank? But young and sexy, of course."

"Nope. Middle-aged and more wrinkled than a 100-year-old fig. No teeth either. And what a voice!"

I could hardly wait.

"What about the voice?"

"Imagine running a piece of broken glass over a sheet of rusty metal and you've got it," said Dooley, chuckling fondly. "Oh boy, what a voice!"

I stared at Dooley in horror and amazement.

"Not Paloma?"

"That's right. Paloma! How did you guess?"

"You must be joking! You're not going to marry Paloma?"

"Marriage? Who said anything about marriage?"

"They are a bit conservative here in the *pueblo*, you know. It's either that or living in sin in Torremolinos or Barcelona."

Dooley managed to inject a trace of scorn in amid the smugness.

"I'm not looking for a wife. I want a maid, somebody to cook a few meals, keep the house shipshape. And I've struck it lucky. I've found a great house and Paloma goes with it. Yep, *hombre*, just plug into the village grapevine and your problems are solved."

Little did he know that his were just beginning. It was not the grapevine he had connected with but a piece of poison ivy. Paloma was the Godmother of the village cleaning women, a shrewd little lady with a rat-trap mind and a heart of flint. She snapped up innocent newcomers to the *pueblo* faster than a cat taking a sparrow. Since newcomers rarely knew the rate for cleaners, Paloma kindly offered them her services at only double the usual charge. That got her inside the door. When the house owners said they were taking a trip, Paloma obligingly offered to keep the place in order during their absence. The take-over was complete.

Paloma had a ringful of keys that she displayed like scalps.

"They know they can trust me. I've never had a complaint yet," she boasted.

True enough. Her clients were terrified. The Godmother ruled them with a rod of iron. Not that Dooley would admit his error at first. Instead he started chuckling. Whenever you met him, he was chuckling.

"Hey, you know what Paloma did this morning? Told me to get out of bed and go for a walk so she could clean the place. At 7.30!"

A few nights later he was in the bar, chuckling again.

"Don't want to go home before 11 and spoil the fun. Paloma asked if she could watch a special programme on my television and guess what? She brought three of her friends along, too. What a character!"

The next night he was in the bar again. When he saw me, he swiftly constructed an expression of cheerful complacency but I had seen the frown that it replaced. Dooley was beginning to crack.

"How much does a packet of washing powder cost?" he asked casually.

"Heck, I don't know."

"Mmm. How about a litre of milk?"

"Maybe 90 pesetas."

"It's just that Paloma always asks for 500 pesetas to buy stuff but there's never any change. Forgetful, I suppose. I think she's used to working for the rich. Last night I went to get some food from the fridge and she had thrown everything out. She says she always chucks out leftovers."

"You've got to keep Paloma in the style to which she is accustomed, you know."

"Of course. But I wish she wouldn't throw out bottles of Bourbon. Half full that last one was."

A few days later I called on Dooley. The smugness was fighting a losing battle. Moody desperation was taking its place, though he tried to conceal it. He attempted a chuckle, but it came out like a sob.

"Listen. Maybe I'm being unfair." he said, then winced at the noise as Paloma banged pots and pans about in the kitchen. He took me out to the terrace.

"I mean Paloma is a fantastic worker—my, how she works. But her standards are so high. Or maybe she doesn't understand me too well. Yesterday for example I told her to leave my room because the papers were all over the place. But when I came back she had cleaned it all out. The place was immaculate, but no papers."

"Important papers?"

"Important? My God, the last chapter of the book. Taken me months to get it right. All gone. Paloma had tossed them all away. Said she thought they were just silly old scribblings."

"Well, she can't read. Otherwise, naturally she would have realised she had a masterpiece in her hands."

Dooley did not appreciate irony. He took a swig of bourbon and I noticed his eyes were bloodshot. He looked wild, hunted, as though he were about to leap off the terrace. He was no longer the Dooley we all knew and tried to avoid.

"Then this morning I went into the top bedroom to finish off some work. I locked the door because you can't be too careful."

Dooley had striven to keep his guilty secret from the *pueblo*. To listen to him, he could charm any woman to his bed, but he feared that the *pueblo*, with its stereotyped ideas, might get the wrong idea if it learned that he spent his spare time clicking away with knitting needles.

"I was there a few minutes when along came Paloma and started rattling the door handle. 'Open up', she yelled. I told her not to disturb me, but she kept banging on the door and demanding to know what I was doing. Most disturbing. Couldn't concentrate at all. And she was listening outside, I'm sure. I could hear her breathing."

"Maybe she was worried about you."

Dooley seized on the explanation.

"That's it. She's so conscientious. I guess I'm lucky to have her."

I tried to explain that the real problem was that Paloma treated tenants as interlopers who had to obey her rules. She assumed that since the owner had given her the key of the house she had proprietorial rights. And since she combined the merciful qualities of Attila the Hun and Genghis Khan he could not expect ...

"Please," interrupted Dooley, "Don't think I cannot handle the situation. Paloma is basically a good-hearted person and we're just having a little misunderstanding. Nothing more. Come and try her cooking. That will convince you."

Before going into the kitchen, however, he knocked back two more glasses of Bourbon. Paloma was there, putting on a performance worthy of an Oscar. Peering through the steam, she curled a contemptuous lip at seeing Dooley don an apron.

"Señor, this is no place for men," she declared, "Cooking is women's business."

Buoyed up by the alcohol, Dooley smiled patronisingly and

replied: "Some of the world's greatest chefs are men and I have been praised by top gourmets for my mayonnaise. It's an art which I happen to have mastered. Just watch."

He began mixing the ingredients, explaining how vital it was to get just the right blend of oil and egg. Paloma sniffed and peeled potatoes. Dooley completed his masterpiece and put the mayonnaise in the fridge. Then we retired to the dining room to await events.

After a plateful of Paloma's clams fried delicately in a kilo or so of garlic came some pork with leaden chips, then a salad. Paloma brought out the mayonnaise and laid it on the table with a theatrical air. Dooley gazed down at the shimmering, glutinous mass in disbelief.

"This isn't what I made," he gasped.

"*Claro que no!*" retorted Paloma triumphantly. "I threw out that rubbish. Men just have no idea. This is the real thing I made myself."

At that moment, every shred of smugness fled from Dooley's bearing. The tycoon beneath the surface came to life. His face went purple. He sprang to his feet and with volcanic wrath advanced on Paloma. For once, she quaked.

"Go!" he thundered, "Go! Go! Go!"

Paloma went, like a frightened rabbit, slamming the door behind her. The campaign was far from over, however. She was still guardian of the house and she still had the key. A few days later Dooley was sighted tramping along the village street, suitcases in hand.

"The Godmother suggested there was another house along here I could rent," he sighed, "It was an offer I couldn't refuse."

18

RAISING THE ROOF

Pablo scratched his head. Antonio shrugged. Placido drifted quietly towards the nearby bar. It was a crisis, no doubt about that. The old mill's walls had been repaired, tons of ancient machinery used to grind corn and sugar cane had been ripped out, new beams had been transported from the remotest corners of the sierras. A few weeks' work had stretched into months, or was it years? All at staggering cost.

Once optimistic and carefree, the mill owner had withered into a mere shell, sustained by brandy and Pablo's promises. And now the roof would not fit. No matter how you looked at it, something had gone seriously wrong.

"An architect! That's what we need," said Pablo.

"Then let's get one. Now!" said the owner, grasping that a real crisis had been reached. An architect. This was a revolutionary idea for a *pueblo* dweller.

"*Tranquilo!*" said Pablo. "I know one. I'll bring him this afternoon. He'll sort it out."

Later that day he returned with a man bearing a briefcase and an air of importance. He smiled patronisingly at the worried owner and set about a professional diagnosis. He examined the building from all angles. He walked inside, climbed up ladders, walked outside, took a tour around the walls. He took out a slide rule and made some calculations. Then he scratched his head.

"The roof won't fit," he said.

"Is this the architect?" asked the owner.

"As good as," replied Pablo. "I couldn't find the architect, so his cousin came along."

Initiative. That is what you need in a builder. So naturally, when the time came to perform some *obras* (building work) on my house, I hired Pablo for the job. I had been putting the moment off for years. But finally the racket from insects chomping away at beams and the showers of debris from the rotting bedroom roof had pushed me into precipitate action.

Besides, the novelty of saying "Hello" to the neighbours every time I wished to clean my teeth or empty my bowels had faded. This was a pity because the journey from bedroom to bathroom had kept both myself and my wife in good shape and extremely alert. It entailed negotiating two flights of steps, going out into the street, dodging passing mules and goats, stumbling over the cobbles, and entering the stable beneath the house. Somewhere beyond the stable lay a flush toilet which, when we installed it, was possibly the only one in our street.

Normal building regulations have never carried much weight in the *pueblo*. None of the dwellings was designed. They just happened, over many centuries. Huddled together as though for protection from Barbary pirates, they form a jigsaw of interlocking rooms, terraces, and intimate family histories. My house and garden border six other properties. Beneath my kitchen lies Pura's living room. Above the bathroom is her spare room. It is best not to fall out with one's neighbours.

Each house leans against the others. Remove one at the lower end of the *pueblo* and the chances are the whole lot would collapse like a row of dominoes. Specialised local knowledge is thus vital before you start tampering with any dwelling. Pablo's architect's cousin would not know Le Corbusier or Frank Lloyd Wright from an Eskimo, but he can squeeze six rooms into a plot the size of a telephone kiosk and still have space to spare.

Knowing that Pablo had all this technological expertise on call,

I decided to entrust a few structural alterations to him. Nothing ambitious, just new floors, new roofs, a few stairways.

"Easy," said Pablo, "I"ll fix up the *permiso*."

Some time later I collected the permit from the town hall. There was something about it that I did not understand.

"Pablo, what's this? All it says here is that I am building a fireplace and altering a window."

"So you are, aren't you?"

"Yes, but what about all the rest?"

Pablo looked at me as though at a backward child.

"*Hombre*, do you want to put the experts to all sorts of trouble, having to come all the way out here to check what you're doing?"

"Not really."

"Do you want some city smart-ass, who knows nothing, to order you to pull the whole place down because he thinks it's unsafe?"

"Certainly not."

"Do you want to pay hundreds of thousands of pesetas for permits and architects?"

"Heaven forbid!"

"Exactly. So you're just changing a window and a few other little things, right?"

Pablo's squad hit the house like a tornado. The old walls, mud and boulders glued together with a couple of centuries of dedicated whitewashing, trembled alarmingly as tiles and worm-eaten beams were wrenched out.

"*No pasa nada*," said Pablo, "We know what we're doing."

I believed him too. Even when one of the bricklayers, resurfacing a wall, cheerfully buried a live wire. It took several hours chipping into the cement to locate it. Even when a new row of shelves listed like the Titanic.

Of course, the bricklayers could have claimed they were in a state of shock. As they removed tiles from the bedroom's crumbling roof, a six-foot snake emerged from the darkest recesses, scattering bricklayers in all directions. On second thoughts, I was the one who should have been in shock, recalling all the nights I had wondered what was causing strange, rustling noises a few inches above my head.

The new roof was to be built in traditional style, with wooden beams, over which would be laid bamboo cane, then tar-paper and finally tiles. The builders and myself headed for the countryside to find some suitable bamboo. Several piles of cut cane were rejected before we finally started stripping the dried-up leaves off some that met our requirements. My worries about the house faded as we worked to the soothing murmur of the crickets and of water flowing along the irrigation channels. The village sat on the ridge above us, sleepy in the heat. Occasionally, the chiming of the church clock reached our ears.

"Just as well that the moon is on the wane," said José, one of the workers, scraping away with his sickle.

"Why's that?"

"Because you can suffer nasty effects if you cut cane at the wrong time. One year I cut fresh cane during the new moon. The sap was rising and I went down with a terrible rash. It nearly killed me."

The *obras* nearly killed *me*, for I foolishly volunteered to help in a bid to speed up the work and cut costs. It was high summer and within half an hour my muscles creaked, sweat drenched my whole body, black shapes swam in front of the eyes.

Pablo and his men worked on, coolly, methodically. Despite the heat they rarely stopped for a drink. The materials were transported up the street by mule and after that everything was carried out by human labour. No luxuries like cement mixers. José was the cement mixer.

Pablo and his team awakened me every morning as they settled like a row of sparrows on the doorstep of the house opposite and gossiped until exactly 8am. Then the work began. Keeping up was impossible.

"No time for looking at the view," cried Pablo, as I wilted after heaving up another load of *mezcla* (cement) and tried to console myself with the thought that I was learning some new technical terms. Some people claim that the Andalusians are lazy, that they have a flair for

fiestas and *flamenco* but not much else. These are the same people who claim that the unemployed don't really want to work or they would find a job. They tend to offer these insights from a place in the shade with an iced gin and tonic to hand.

Pablo and his men did not have time to argue with that point of view. They did not stop to complain about the government or the cost of living. They just worked steadily, six days a week. So new shelves collapsed the first time I put any weight on them. So they put the large window frame in the small window cavity and the small frame in the large window space. But they worked, my, how they worked.

Even so, it was a pity about the floor. We had planned to raise the living room floor so as to give adequate headroom in the room beneath it, the old stable. But, after the new concrete beams had been installed and the concrete had been poured and had set like, well, like concrete, I noticed that the floor was no higher. It seemed a point worth raising with Pablo. He maintained a poker face, the one he reserved for nit-picking clients.

"I forgot," he told me.

Anybody can make mistakes. Like El Moreno, especially El Moreno. Muscles like marble columns. And cheerful? Never stopped smiling. Which is what he did when I pointed out there was something wrong with the steps he was building in the patio. Judging by his starting point and the size of each step, it appeared that the stairs might end up giving access to the first floor instead of the ground floor.

"These steps are wrong," I warned.

El Moreno grinned, shrugged and added another step.

"Pablo, quick, get down here," I called.

Before Pablo had materialised, another step had been set in place.

"Stop him," I cried.

"What exactly is the problem?" asked Pablo, as El Moreno sloshed down more mezcla and more bricks.

"Ah, I see, you want the steps to start back there."

Another step.

"*Sí, sí.* We"ll have to do this lot again. *No pasa nada.*"

A flourish from El Moreno and another step was finished.

We stopped him in the end. He grinned, went back to the bottom and started building the steps again. Another bricklayer was rebuilding the sloping shelves. Pablo was rebuilding the fireplace that had somehow got damaged. There was nothing to be done about the floor. Tempers were fraying. The *obras* seemed to have gone on for months. They *had* gone on for months. The house seemed destined to be full forever of cement and sand and tramping feet and hammering and dust. In the garden, buried under old beams and other debris, one miserable melon struggled to survive. Dust-covered neighbours were turning surly.

Pablo and I had started good friends. The beautiful relationship was coming to an end. If I made one more complaint, it looked as though he would explode. If he said "*No pasa nada*" to me once more, I would.

For days on end each of us in turn chipped away at a rock at the foot of a staircase. It was too risky to use a pneumatic drill but the rock had to go if there was to be sufficient headroom. In future, I was determined I would be able to walk through the house without constantly banging my head or bending nearly double. Since Pablo was not much more than knee-high to a *burro*, he could not understand this obsession with headroom and frequently demonstrated to me how easily he could pass through a doorway.

At last, however, the rock was removed. Or most of it. Or some of it. Anyway, a compromise was reached. A compromise was reached on almost everything. Anything to finish the *obras*. Pablo and his men packed up and went off to torment another house. I paid the bill. The work was done. The house was swept and mopped about 15 times, white-washed, painted. It looked great. Until I lit a fire and the smoke seeped out through a large crack in the bedroom wall.

"*No pasa nada*," said Pablo. "Is normal, *hombre*. It just needs a bit of plaster inside the chimney."

No problems with the roof. The cane had been nailed in place and covered with asphalt paper and cement and tiles. Nothing could penetrate that. Except rain.

"Is normal," said Pablo. "New roofs always leak. You see it takes time for them to settle down when they are on old walls."

"But this isn't an old wall. It is a new one and it is leaking, too."

"Is normal. You always get the same problem with new walls. After a week or so the rain will have swollen the cement and stopped any more water coming in. *No pasa nada*."

At least you can now walk through the house without stooping. Plenty of headroom everywhere. Except where the stable was and they forgot to raise the ceiling. Except in the only doorway where previously I had no trouble. Now I bang my head there every time. Perhaps Pablo's architect's cousin can explain that one to me.

19

AN ENGLISHMAN'S HOME

A new bar opened in the village and it was a surprise to everybody. Unlike the traditional establishments, with their zinc counters and harsh strip lighting and tasty displays of nude girls leering from road haulier's calendars, this one consisted of a couple of dark, beamed rooms with tables and chairs and, no matter what the temperature was outside, a fire blazing in one corner. Anybody entering was courteously offered a seat, while the proprietor searched for a drink in one of the wall cupboards. Most surprising of all, considering the *pueblo's* distance from the sea, was the place's name: The Yacht Club.

It was run by an Englishman, an Englishman of the old school. Don Carlos made no concessions to climate or local customs. He dressed in the manner of an English country squire, sturdy walking shoes, cavalry twill trousers, thick tweed jacket, checked woollen shirt and tie. Inside or outside, day or night, he never removed his trilby hat. He was an affable type but painfully introverted, a man of few words in any language. Although he and his aging parents had lived many years in the country, they remained as stubbornly British in their ways as somebody who had never left the Home Counties.

Carlos's father had the military bearing appropriate to a former officer in the Indian Army, but now in retirement, like many of those who had served the Raj, he had nowhere to go. The Old Country was out of the question, it had changed so much. He was used to sub-tropical heat, to steamy monsoon months, to cool hill stations, to a stiffly formal world of chota pegs, polo and respectful servants. There was no going home. So the family had come to Spain, where the natives were friendly and the chill did not enter into your bones. The whole family seemed like melancholy relics from the Edwardian age, always correctly attired, genteel, polite to a fault, and totally out of place. Carlos had attended the best public schools and was equipped with a fine upper-class accent but little else to allow him to handle the problems of everyday life. He apparently had never held a job.

The family scraped by on its army pension, but the cash appeared to be running out for they expended little on luxuries or indeed on food, although they did spend an alarming amount on wine and whisky. Eventually the parents died and Carlos, a sadly lonely figure, lost all restraint in his drinking habits. More and more frequently, he drank himself into oblivion, though even to the last, before he slid beneath the table, he managed to keep a stiff upper lip. His comatose form was regularly carried home by tolerant villagers. Soon he was selling off the antiques and anything else of value from the family home. When he appeared one day waving an ancient pistol, the neighbours ran for cover and called the Civil Guard. Carlos thought it was a merry joke, not realising how close he came to a sudden demise. It made little difference, however. He had the air of a doomed man and, shortly after, he was found dead, whether from neglect, alcohol, or other causes, nobody really knew. The Yacht Club, which had never had a licence to operate, floated off into the sunset.

The saga of Carlos and his unusual life style hardly raised any eyebrows among the locals. Though they had limited knowledge of "*los ingleses*," they subscribed to the myth that they were all "*caballeros*" (this was before so-called lager louts wrought havoc in Spanish coastal resorts and on England's image). They also understood that English gentlemen tended to be, not to put too fine a point on it, a little strange in their ways.

Their view, after all, was confirmed by the actions of three other expatriates in our midst, a trio who, when you came to think about it, were exactly the sort of clients Carlos was hoping The Yacht

Club would attract. No three persons could have been more different in character than Don Alberto, Don Roberto, and Don Eduardo.

The health food fad had been the making of Don Alberto. He had finally sold his chain of stores at a handy price and used some of the cash to buy a house in Spain. His ruddy complexion and white beard gave him a jovial, Father Christmas-like appearance, which was somewhat deceiving. Organically grown vegetables and muesli for breakfast may be good for your health but they had done nothing to mellow Alberto. When something got his goat, he would explode into spectacular anger.

In contrast, Don Roberto's forte was icy disdain. Having made a million in construction, he knew just how to build a wall around himself to exclude interlopers and avoid any social intercourse.

Finally there was Don Eduardo, urbane and sociable and a born gossip. His background was shrouded in mystery, although it clearly had nothing to do with muesli or bricks. The fact that he was fluent in Spanish set him apart from many expatriates who seemed to take pride in their ignorance of the lingo; apparently they feared that if they acquire any fluency chaps might say they'd "gone native".

The three did have two things in common, however. They all lived in spacious, converted mills in the hills above the *pueblo*. And they were all English. Naturally, they never spoke to one another. In the style that legend associates with English gentry, they were comfortably off, carried themselves with an air of authority, and had eccentric tastes. Who else would want to cut themselves off from the world in such an inconvenient, isolated spot?

Until the Civil War, the mills had functioned on water power, grinding everything from corn to sugar-cane. Then they had fallen into disuse, the walls had crumbled and nobody had the cash or the inclination to repair them. Until the arrival of Don Alberto, Don Roberto, and Don Eduardo. They had bought the mills at peppercorn prices, undismayed, in fact charmed, by the fact that there were no roads to their properties. The only access was on foot or on a mule's back. Thus the work of conversion moved slowly and teams of mules and donkeys were needed to haul the bricks and cement up to the mills.

Blasting was necessary too to cut foundations for new rooms. This got Don Eduardo into hot water. His explosives expert seemed to know his job as he bored into the rock, set charges, covered them with rubber tyres to muffle the shock waves, and retreated to a safe position. Initially all went well, but then came an error of calculation. A tremendous explosion echoed around the hills and shook the village window panes. Lumps of rock soared skywards and fell to earth, directly on to the roof of the Civil Guard headquarters. The Guards rushed outside, clutching their guns and looking anxiously around for the Rojos who had picked the *pueblo* to re-start the Civil War.

Profound apologies and offers to pay for any damage were necessary to restore good relations. Don Eduardo was up to it; not only had he an easy charm and a good knowledge of vernacular Spanish, he had once worked in the diplomatic service. That is to say he had occupied an office in various British embassies and consulates. He had been "in intelligence". This of course was top secret.

I had read enough spy novels to know when to keep my lip buttoned. In Eduardo's presence, therefore, I tried not to let on that I knew about his past. They wouldn't get me to talk. Discretion was my middle name. But not, it soon turned out, Eduardo's. If there was one thing he liked to reminisce about it was his career in espionage. After a few brandies, he would launch into accounts of funny business in Gibraltar or Algiers, while I looked anxiously around, expecting somebody from Scotland Yard to emerge from the woodwork and clamp us all in irons.

As one would expect from a master of deception, Don Eduardo was hard to pin down. Just when he was approaching an important point, he would chuckle and say: "Yes, but that's another story."

He was full of bright ideas for boosting his income—apparently spies do not have a very generous social security system. His efforts to export little-heard-of Spanish wines to England went down the plughole. A project to cover the coast with bowling greens somehow did not click; most Spaniards had never heard of the pastime and those who had no doubt recalled tales of that pirate Drake and how, according to English history, he insisted on finishing his game of bowls before sinking the dastardly Spanish Armada.

Don Eduardo was a good raconteur and, when he was inspired by a brainwave, he liked to share it.

"Do you know why all the Brits suffer from piles?" he might ask without warning. "I've been thinking about it and it's obvious. They don't use bidets. The French always wash their private parts with cold water after going to the toilet, and they don't have piles. That's the answer, you see, the cold water. But the Brits, stupid buggers, never learn. By the way, where was I? Ah yes, about Peter Ustinov's father—amazing character—when he was doing a bit of work for us in Lisbon... mmm, but that's another story... "

I soon realised that, like many espionage agents, Don Eduardo craved recognition. What's the point of being a spy, if you can't boast about your exploits afterwards? He was, he said, planning a book and hinted at spicy revelations. He had, after all, been a close associate of such notorious characters as Kim Philby, who had penetrated the highest levels of British intelligence before fleeing to Moscow. Peering at Eduardo over a third or fourth brandy, I couldn't help wondering whether his lapses into vagueness and his fund of anecdotes were part of an elaborate smokescreen.

Philby's defection had followed that of two other notorious ex-Cambridge University recruits to Communism, Maclean and Burgess, and there was continuing speculation about who the "fourth" or the "fifth man" might be, meaning another double agent embedded in the British establishment. During his career, "turning" agents and deceiving the enemy with misinformation had been Don Eduardo's speciality and he too had been at Cambridge in the Thirties. It did make you wonder.

As it turned out, Don Eduardo was indeed harbouring a considerable secret. One day a glib young specialist in espionage tales tracked him down and, after a good lunch, Eduardo spilled the beans. He knew the whereabouts of a legendary double agent who may well have changed the course of World War Two by misleading the Germans about the precise location of the Allied landings in France. Everybody believed that this agent had died 40 years earlier, but Eduardo knew differently. His visitor pricked up his ears, casually asked how the man might be contacted, and rushed off to sell the information for a hefty amount to the British media. Unfortunately, there was no recognition in it for Eduardo and no cash either.

At first Don Eduardo was on good terms with Don Roberto. They were said to have gone to school together. At any rate, he was one of the few local residents with whom Roberto conversed. Roberto quickly made it known that he did not wish to attend public or private functions. He was not eager to make friends with local society. Bridge-playing expatriates who staggered up to his hilltop eyrie in a state of collapse and expected to be greeted with tea and sympathy were firmly rebuffed. Anybody presenting their card had it firmly handed back. Roberto sought privacy and repose.

He carried this policy to surprising extremes, being known to make a detour rather than acknowledge somebody's existence by speaking to them. "Private. No Entry" signs soon made his point doubly clear on a path leading through his grounds. Not that the villagers paid much attention, continuing to use the path as they had since the days of the Great Armada. When the English lords started erecting fences too, however, they were not over-pleased.

"Nobody has ever built a fence around here, because there's nothing worth stealing out in the campo," growled Miguel, my neighbour. "If anybody's hungry and wants a fig or a tomato, well, they're welcome to take one. Of course, in the past, you could expect a beating if the Civil Guards caught you. But nobody thought of putting a fence around his *finca*."

The *ingleses*, however, seemed bent on confirming the stereotyped opinions of the locals. *Los ingleses* were "gentlemen," but they were also eccentric, stuffy and stubbornly possessive. Look at the way they clung to a useless bit of rock like Gibraltar, which was rightfully Spanish.

Soon, as if to confirm the *pueblo's* ideas, there was trouble up at mill. Don Eduardo and Don Roberto agreed that they should construct a road to serve their properties. It was a costly and difficult project as the road had to zig-zag up a cliff. Work began and the road began climbing the hill, but halfway up it came to an abrupt halt. Don Eduardo and Don Roberto had fallen out over the project. An icy chill settled over the hillside and the mills remained isolated. Their proprietors lived within a few hundred metres of one another, but they contrived to ignore one another's existence.

Don Alberto kept aloof from all this, but he had his own difficulties. He had a heart of gold, but was a little... er... temperamental. He too had ingrained ideas about private property, which inevitably created friction. One afternoon a family with young children lost their way as they climbed up from the riverbed below Alberto's mill. The hillside grew steeper and rockier until they were close to desperation. Finally, scratched, dishevelled, and exhausted, they reached a corner of Don Alberto's garden and prepared to climb over the wall. At that moment a whiskery, crimson face came into view, peering down at them. At last, a fellow Englander to the rescue.

"*Gracias a Dios!* We're so glad to see you, Alberto," they cried.

The glowering apparition turned a deeper shade of red. "Back!" he roared. "Back! Don't you know this is private property? You can't pass through here."

Another event to disturb Alberto's Shangri-la occurred when he was absent. Film-makers decided that the landscape around the *pueblo* was ideal for a drama supposed to be located in some violent South American republic. Household names appeared briefly in our streets, the villagers were entertained by the antics of the film crew, and substantial sums of cash flowed into one or two local pockets. Then peace returned.

Shortly afterwards so did Don Alberto, and war broke out. Comfortably back in his mill, sipping his aperitif, he gazed out at the pleasing view and almost dropped his drink.

"What the devil is that? What's been going on?" he gasped.

For one scene the film-makers had needed a cave. As there was not one handy, they found an overhang of rock and built plastic and papier maché walls, painting them to simulate rock. It was an ingenious piece of work and looked authentic enough on film, but the weather had been at work and by the time Alberto returned, the flimsy structure had become a sad apology for a cave. Indeed the crumbling plastic and cardboard affair had become a positive eyesore. Unfortunately, it was located slap opposite his house.

"What's this monstrosity! Outrageous!" blazed Don Alberto. And he marched across to the structure and ripped it down. A few days later the municipal policeman was on his doorstep with Felix, a goatherd. Felix was highly aggrieved.

"That cave was sheltering my goats," he said. "And it was on

my land. You had no right to touch it. I want a new shelter."

Swallowing his wrath, Don Alberto was forced to pay compensation. Soon it was his turn to fall out with Don Roberto. Alberto liked to sit out on his terrace and survey the view, while listening to the waters thundering along the irrigation channel. Tapped from the river way up in the mountains, the water flowed along a concrete channel pinned to the mountainside. Above the mill, it changed direction and plunged down with great force. The waterwheel had gone, but every night the reservoir near Alberto's mill was filled and every morning the irrigation guardian would come along to open the sluices to direct the water to one or other part of the countryside. Water distribution was strictly controlled by the irrigation board according to the size of each farmer's land and the fees he paid. The complex system was said to date back to the time of the Moors and it worked with impressive precision.

That was something Don Alberto could appreciate as he sat back sipping a cup of tea and stroking his beard. But one evening he almost choked when he gazed out from his mill. At considerable expense, he and several farmers had constructed a dirt track to serve their fields and his mill, previously accessible only by mule path. Don Roberto had been asked to participate but had coldly declined. The work had gone ahead anyway and "Private road" signs had been erected to keep out interlopers. What was Alberto's surprise when he saw that a strange vehicle was parked on the track.

He hurried down to his faithful handyman's shack.

"Antonio, whose is that machine over there?"

"Why, Don Alberto, that belongs to Don Roberto."

"Roberto? Confounded cheek! And after he refused to come in with us! I'll stop that."

Alberto proceeded to block any exit by parking his own car across the track, muttering: "He's got in, but damned if he's going to get out."

Next day, Roberto walked over from his mill to pick up his car and found his way out blocked. It was the moment Alberto had been waiting for. He stormed forth to do battle and the two Englishmen engaged in a fierce argument. Threats and insults flew as the *campesinos* looked on in bewilderment. The battle raged on, Roberto and Alberto firing a salvo of angry letters at one another. Then Roberto ended the campaign with a master-stroke, simply buying an entire hilltop, which gave him the right of access to Alberto's road. At vast cost, he extended the road through his own property. Alberto accepted the inevitable and the English *caballeros* made peace over cocktails in their Spanish castles.

Roberto's coup did provoke some debate in the *pueblo*, however, for the hill was not any old hill, but the one on which was located the crumbling traces of the old Moorish fortress. Some trouble-makers suggested it was a disgrace that a national monument should fall into alien hands, but nobody was prepared to put their hands in their pockets and that was the problem—there was no public money available to buy the fortress.

Soon, Roberto had a new neighbour and a new antagonist.

Don Eduardo sold his mill and moved to a new hideaway. In his place came a family of Swedish and Russian descent, oblivious to the quagmire of rivalries and tensions they had stumbled into. Naively, they inquired through their gardener if they might use Roberto's road to bring some furniture to their property. Given to understand that there was no problem, they went ahead.

But they had made a fatal error. It seemed that Don Roberto himself had not been consulted, and he had not built a highway to his door for the use of any Antonio, Dick, or Ivan. In a cold fury, he stormed over to his new neighbour's mill and handed him a letter, curtly declaring: "I advise you to read this."

The missive proved to have explosive qualities, unleashing a crushing lecture on moral values. It harangued the offender with charges of perfidy, duplicity, and everything short of child molesting. "Obviously," Don Roberto wrote, with bewildering sarcasm, "the clocks run differently east of Vienna."

On the hillside above the *pueblo* the battle lines were drawn once again. That, however, as Don Eduardo would say, is another story.

20

PRINCE OF PRACTICANTES

While the English were acting in character, the American representative in the *pueblo* was doing his best to live up to his nation's stereotype. Dooley had always been a generous type. Always ready to share. His contacts with the famous, for example. He had never been mean about those, supplying the *pueblo* with anecdotes of his intimate relations with presidents and filmstars. It seemed he had been on first-name terms with half of Hollywood and most of Washington. You had to be a cheerless cynic to question his endless stories. After all he came from the fabled US of A, with which we were all intimately acquainted thanks to film and television.

Too bad that, in equally magnanimous mood, he also insisted on sharing details of his many afflictions, at every opportunity. He was free with details, of his sore throat, aching joints, stomach upsets and many other life-threatening afflictions, none of which seemed to jibe with his appearance. For he looked the eternal teenager, disgustingly healthy, lean and carefully tanned.

Dooley never told you how old he was, nor what precisely he had done in his glamorous past life. There were hints of high executive positions, which never quite tallied with his reluctance to pay for a drink. Now he was a Writer and a determined hispanophile. You could tell because he was always referring to "Hem" and bullfighting and dwelling on the torture of being creative. And when he became a Sick Writer he was even more generous with his information.

"It must be this *pueblo* diet. I should have stuck to steak," he moaned. "It's okay if you've lived all your life on garbanzos and goats' milk. But hell, I'm a Philadelphia boy."

So why didn't he fly straight home to cellophane-wrapped cheeseburgers and all-American hygiene, someone inquired hopefully.

"With hospital beds at 500 dollars a day? Are you crazy?"

He had to find a doctor. For a few seconds he considered visiting our *pueblo médico*, but quickly discarded the idea. He had nothing against him on professional grounds. Dooley just felt a doctor should make house calls. Since the village was pinned to a mountainside, most of the streets required acrobatic skills to negotiate them. We should have been allocated a mountaineer. Instead we got Don Ignacio whose gout was so bad that he could hardly budge from his surgery. No way was he going to tackle those streets.

A steady stream of arthritic cripples, wheezing pneumonia victims, and grey-faced cardiac cases tottered down the precipitous cobbles to his place. A fair percentage survived, demonstrating how good exercise was for you.

Dooley felt his ailment was worthy of more expensive attention, so he took himself to a doctor in the next *pueblo*, a man of august presence and held in wide esteem. Not being a good listener, Dooley had not learned that the good doctor's prestige was due to his ability to produce children rather than to any sick bed expertise.

Dooley came back loaded with packages and chuckling to himself.

"The guy's an artist," he said. "Look at these pictures he drew me. What a sense of humour!"

The pictures all seemed to show rabbits in mating positions. The humour was not immediately apparent.

"Yes, but what's wrong with you?"

Dooley looked surprised, as though he had never thought to ask.

"I'm not quite clear on that. But I gotta take these pills, the red ones like torpedoes, three times a day. And the blue ones, like Easter eggs, twice a day. And then I have to have injections every six hours.

That should fix it."

That should fix anything, I thought.

I next saw Dooley two days later. He was standing outside the church gripping the railing. I waved as I passed. When I came back two hours later, he was still there.

"This girl Mercedes," he said, "Do you think she knows what she's doing?"

"Come and have a coffee and we'll talk about it."

"You must be joking," said Dooley, his face contorted. "I can't move. I can hardly walk. I've been stuck here all morning."

With the aid of a few bystanders, I guided him home where we laid him on his bed—face down.

"But didn't you know about Mercedes?"

Mercedes strode importantly about the village, exercising the duties of a *practicante*, the equivalent of a district nurse. Her symbol of prestige was a little black bag, which she opened to reveal a fearsome display of instruments. Most fearsome of all was the large syringe, with needles that should have been in the British Museum. Despite intensive practice, she had never quite mastered the art of giving injections. I had known people to visit her for an infected arm and be unable to sit down for a week.

"She's trained, isn't she?" asked Dooley, whimpering a little.

"In a manner of speaking."

"What do you mean?"

"Mercedes has never actually qualified. It's her boyfriend who is the *practicante*. But Mercedes has known him for years. And she's a sharp girl, so she must have learned something."

Dooley's tan was not looking good.

"You should have said you wanted the best," I told him. "Ricardo's your man. Sheer artistry."

Ricardo was a prince among *practicantes*. No matter how many hours he worked there were always more patients queuing up for his jabs. Like all artists, though, he did tend to be temperamental. When Ricardo told you to expect him at a certain time, you didn't quibble if

he was four hours late. As his fame spread, so had he become more of a prima donna. But nobody complained. He was a professional from the tips of his toes to the end of his finely-honed needle.

Perhaps, years ago, it was not like that. Who knows how many sore buttocks testified to the agony of apprenticeship? During his career Ricardo must have seen more trembling flesh than Rubens knew existed. But in the end—what a performance. Speed and confidence were the secrets. Deft, methodical preparations. A sharp smack. In went the needle. The syringe was inserted. Zip went the plunger. And that was it. Smooth as old brandy. And no pain, no pain at all.

Dooley swiftly switched his allegiance to Ricardo and within a few days he was hooked, just like the rest of the *pueblo*. Antibiotics were as much part of the local diet as corn flakes and sauerkraut elsewhere. Tranquillizers and sleeping pills were especially popular among housewives suffering from a common affliction they referred to as "*nervios.*" Without their daily fix of pills, jabs, and suppositories, the hardy, robust countryfolk would have come to a standstill. The discarded phials, plastic containers, and bottles that ended up in my garden testified to the demand. Quite a few of them were sown by my neighbour Caridad who lived up to her name by puncturing her young children at every opportunity.

But Dooley would not listen to warning stories. Whenever I saw him, he was either queuing up at the pharmacy or staggering home laden with more medical supplies. He became a pharmaceutical expert, exchanging experiences with his neighbours, swapping boxes of pills and bottles containing bizarre liquids. It was no longer possible to have a sensible conversation in Dooley's presence. Attempt to compare the quality of a Rioja with a Valdepeñas and Dooley would quickly change the subject to the relative merits of the latest vintage penicillin and Brand X. He had become a junkie. Fortunately, after months of treatment that cost Dooley the equivalent of a new hospital wing back home, he claimed to feel better.

"Things are looking up. Except that I've started getting these dizzy spells," he reported as he gulped back a few pre-lunch capsules.

"And this sore throat. Let's go to the pharmacy and see what they can do."

By now the pharmacist was an old friend and quickly laid out a fine array of pain-killers and germ-fighters on the counter.

"How about this one?" he suggested, offering an impressive packet. "Very effective and only 600 pesetas."

Dooley studied the instructions.

"But these are suppositories. I've got a sore throat."

With a few explicit gestures, the pharmacist indicated that to get to the seat of a problem you did not always have to take the most direct route. Then seeing Dooley's shocked expression, he shrugged and offered him another cure.

"That's better. Only 350 pesetas this one. To be taken three times a day," said Dooley. "I remember reading something about this in The Lancet or the Medical Guide. The latest stuff. Wait a minute, though, what's this? 'Side effects—nausea, dizziness, irritability'. No thanks, I've got those already."

I picked up a small plainly wrapped packet marked "Throat Lozenges".

"How about these?"

"Fifty pesetas?" scoffed Dooley, "How can they be any good at that price? And there's nothing in them, no tetracyline, no codeine, no penicillin, nothing to cause nausea, insomnia or dizziness. What sort of medicine is that?"

"But they *are* for a sore throat."

Reluctantly he bought them. The pharmacist consoled him with the promise that he would certainly have some new lines in next day. But next day Dooley's sore throat was gone.

"It's enough to undermine your faith in medical science," he admitted, as he hurried off to his usual appointment with Ricardo.

21

DEMOCRACY AT WORK

After the Generalísimo died and politics came to the *pueblo*, even the simplest of words or actions tended to be judged ideologically.

"You want this new window in the centre of the wall, I suppose?" said the builder who seemed to have taken up permanent residence in my house. "No," I replied, "More to the left."

He reacted sharply.

"The left? How did they get into this? *Hombre*, there's too much of this political nonsense. People should work more and talk less. That's my opinion—not that I support any of the parties."

All the same, when I came back I saw that the window had been placed just right of centre.

The first general elections since before the Civil War had been an entertaining novelty, but Madrid was so far away that nobody really thought the results could make much difference to their lives. However, when the date for municipal elections was announced, political debate reached fever pitch.

Only a few old-timers could recall the last time parties had campaigned freely for candidates for the local council. That had been back in 1933. Or was it 1934? The council elected had been leftwing. Or was it rightwing? At any rate, it had incurred the wrath of the trade unionists, who on one occasion had invaded the town hall, forcing councillors to leap out of the windows and flee for their lives.

Although, after so many years, the villagers were a little hazy about how to proceed, this did not deter informed debate. There was a good deal of this in the village bars, where the faceless *señoritos* of Madrid were regularly scourged for the poor prices tomatoes were fetching. That was one of the few points on which everybody agreed. Otherwise dialogue and compromise were hard to find. Political allegiances were cheerfully claimed and disclaimed on grounds that the solemn pollsters could never imagine.

"What this country needs is a proletarian revolution," said Benito, who had studied the life of Lenin. "Then everybody could have his own plot of land."

"What this country needs is a 28-year-old Franco," declared Eusebio, who had rapidly expanding business interests. "Then we would have discipline and organisation, like they have in the Soviet Union."

"Look at that!" Manolo the baker was pointing out into the street where two mongrels were busy fornicating. "In the street! In front of women and children! That's what you get with democracy."

Melchor, whose sight was not so good, tried to pound the bar but missed.

"What this country needs is another *alcalde* like Don Calixto. He never meddled in other people's business. And he could tell a good joke, too."

But there were no volunteers to follow in the jokey ex-mayor's fascist footsteps and his favourite tune, the Nationalist anthem *Cara al Sol*, had gone out of fashion.

Even the church had suffered a transformation. A succession of priests had passed through the *pueblo* and left, changed men all. Easygoing Don Santiago had been well-liked, but had been shifted away after one of his parishioners became pregnant. Don Raimundo was very popular with goodlooking teenagers of both sexes, so popular that he was quickly posted elsewhere. Don Diego lost his faith, found a wife, and gave up the priesthood. Don Gregorio, stern and humourless, dwelled long on man's duty and woman's weakness. His inquisitorial qualities so endeared him to the *pueblo* that the bishop quickly called him back to the provincial capital to serve on an ecclesiastical court.

Then came Red Paco. Unlike Gregorio, he rarely donned a cassock or dog collar. Young and casually dressed, he represented a new revolutionary breed in the priesthood. He had once been jailed for cracking an anti-Franco joke in public and, while the younger generation considered Paco a breath of fresh air, he soon established a reputation among more conservative elements as a dangerous subversive.

"The church has to be on the side of social justice. Christ was involved in politics—that's why they killed him," declared Paco, lecturing the villagers on civil liberties, on women's rights, on the need to organise themselves to protect their interests. He formed a youth club and introduced a guitar accompaniment to attract youngsters to church services. Traditionalists were scandalised and they were further shocked when, during a dance in the church plaza, the priest joined in with an exuberant jig of his own. At the annual *romería*, parishioners gaped in amazement at the lorry bearing the image of San Antonio. It and the vehicle were decorated with the colours of Andalusia, which happened to be the same as those of the Andalucistas, a leftwing regional party.

"*Por Dios!*" muttered the older residents, "This is too much. Why can't Paco be like the other priests, chasing the village girls or the village boys? That's what you expect from priests. But this political business isn't right."

As the time approached for the elections, tension increased. The *pueblo* was split between the Andalucistas, led by Benito, the practicante, and the centre-right faction, the Centristas, led by Faustino. Most people were as confused as Pura, our octogenarian neighbour, about the issues and the parties.

"What do you think? Who should I vote for?" she asked me anxiously. But the next day she looked relieved. "It's all right. I know what to do now. They sent me this paper form to explain it."

She showed me a mock voting form from one of the parties, on which their candidates had been firmly marked with an "X".

Tempers rose, threats were hurled. There were plenty of assassinations, though only of opponents' characters.

The rightwingers whispered that Benito had been attracting votes by offering to give free injections. His opponents, it was claimed, could expect only a blunt needle. Ghosts of the past were raised by speculating about the fearful consequences should the "Reds" get in. Benito's appearance did not help him in this respect. Revolutionary zeal emanated from him. With his beard, violent gestures, and his fierce rhetoric, he looked like a cross between Trotsky and the Ayatollah.

Faustino, in contrast, had a distinguished air. His term as mayor during the Franco regime had won him both supporters and enemies. Earnest and somewhat pedantic, he tended to lecture the villagers, a trait which was not always appreciated. After all, he had tried to stop them singing in the bars; it was hard to forget that. And, alleged Benito, he was bullying old people into voting for him by threatening to have their pensions cut off if they did not.

"It's a vote of fear," asserted Benito. "Lots of people daren't vote against the rightwingers who control the town hall. A small group has always decided everything in private. But their day is done."

As it turned out, however, the villagers were more afraid of Benito than his rival. The results were declared at midnight to an expectant crowd in the tiny schoolroom that served as a polling station. The Communists, composed mainly of the richer families' university-educated sons, came nowhere. Victory went to Faustino and his men. Benito and his boys took the rest of the seats.

"It's a *pucherazo* (a fiddle)," cried Benito.

War was soon declared over water rights. Even in the driest years, the *pueblo* usually had enough to drink as water came gushing down in abundance from the mountains. However, during the summer months when the flow diminished, the fields could sometimes only be irrigated once every two weeks. Water was precious and the presence of Vitoriano on the council aroused suspicion.

Vitoriano had big ideas. On a stretch of stony hillside where nothing ever grew he had planted villas and reaped a fortune. Sunstruck foreigners had handed him bundles of cash. It certainly beat planting potatoes and Victor dreamed of becoming a real estate tycoon. He planned to build more houses. The only problem was that the taps in his houses were dry. He had no water.

Vitoriano had never shown much interest in politics, but suddenly just before the elections he had popped up as a firm supporter of the Centristas. When the council announced plans to pump water to a new deposit below the village, Benito's followers put two and two together and quickly came to 10.

"That's our water they're giving away," they declared. "We're going to run short just so strangers living in luxury can fill their swimming pools. It's a scandal."

Searching for documentary proof of his allegations, Benito entered the town hall one day and started searching through the records. Faustino protested at what he regarded as outrageous conduct and called on the *municipal*—the mild-mannered village policeman who found it difficult even to administer a parking ticket—to eject him.

Benito saved himself and the policeman embarrassment by making a strategic retreat. He hurried off to seek reinforcements. Half an hour later the Andalucistas came storming back in strength, but the *alcalde* had moved fast. The town hall doors had been locked and the staff had gone home for the day. Benito and his men marched away, fuming.

Faustino's simmering battle with Paco the priest was next to burst into the open. Paco thundered regularly from the pulpit about the injustices suffered by the workers and suggested that Faustino was out to help not "the people" but the bloated *caciques* (landlords). It was rousing stuff, although talk of *caciques* did not quite fit our *pueblo* where there were no large land-owners and few families without at least a plot of land to support them. More conservative members of the congregation disapproved of Paco's propaganda and boycotted his services.

At Easter the conflict reached boiling point. Posters appeared around the village, appealing for justice and *pan y trabajo* (bread and work) for the oppressed unemployed. The mayor knew who had organised this campaign and at whom it was directed. He ordered the posters removed on the grounds that they had not been properly registered and their source was not identified, as the law required.

"Anti-constitutional! Anti-democratic! Anti-Christian!" protested the priest, and planned a response.

After the final procession on Good Friday, one of the most solemn and most venerated acts of the year, the whole village gathered in the early hours of the morning in the church plaza to listen to a closing oration. This was usually a formality, a call for Christians to make sure that Christ had not died in vain. This time, however, angry currents were circulating. Almost as soon as the young leader of the religious brotherhoods began speaking, murmurs arose. He spoke out fiercely against those who sought to trample the rights of the people. Posters had been ripped down in a way that could only be described as "dictatorial and anti-Christian." Paco nodded approvingly in the background.

"This is nothing to do with *Semana Santa*!" cried a voice, which sounded suspiciously like that of the mayor's wife. "You are talking politics! You are disobeying the Pope. You have no right to meddle in politics."

Others joined in.

"This is a religous ceremony, not a political meeting! Out, out, out!"

Youngsters rallied to the speaker's support.

"Quiet! Let him speak! Out with the fascists!"

"Shut up! You're the fascists! Keep politics out of the church!"

The Civil Guards fingered their gun-butts and looked at one another uncertainly. Passions were running dangerously high. A group of women began singing: "*Viva la Virgen*, our Patron, who has her altar in our breasts." In the end, the ceremony broke up in confusion and the villagers slowly dispersed in angrily arguing groups.

Fortunately, Faustino had stayed away, preferring to remain in a nearby bar rather than view Paco lording it on the church steps. Next day, however, the mayor toured the village in a loudspeaker van, declaring that the truth of the controversy would be known soon enough. "Listen to the radio this afternoon," boomed the loudspeaker. "The mayor has been interviewed and he will explain why he had to act because of trouble-making elements in our community."

Excitement mounted as the time for the broadcast approached. It was not often that the village made news, either on the radio or in the press. The whole *pueblo* tuned in to the advertised programme, but the broadcast proved to be a disappointing anti-climax. "We interviewed the *cura* and we interviewed the *alcalde*," said the

announcer, clearly reeling under the avalanche of passionate opinion from both sides. "But so delicate is the situation that we do not want to do anything to exacerbate it and we have decided not to broadcast their comments."

The language in council debates was often highly incendiary too. After interminable arguments, the final vote on virtually every issue was made on party lines. Faustino tried to cut down the opportunities to speak, claiming it would save time, to which the opposition replied: "This is not democracy."

They vowed revenge and soon enough the opportunity arose. The question of whether or not to chop down a tree became an explosive political issue. The Affair of El Pino dragged on for weeks, everybody taking sides, accusations flying. It began when the Centristas proposed knocking off the corner of a house to allow a street to be widened. Naturally, the Andalucistas opposed such a move.

"Ridiculous!" they charged. "That's somebody's home. Why not just cut down the tree on the other side of the street?"

"Sacrilege!" exclaimed the mayor and his men. "Too many trees have been massacred already. That one stays."

Faustino had become something of a champion of trees. He was particularly proud of the new bypass, where scores of young saplings and palm trees had been planted. One night somebody poured petrol into the hollow trunk of a fine old carob tree near the bypass and set fire to it. The smouldering trunk provoked glee in one half of the *pueblo* and anger in the other. Faustino seethed, for the act of vandalism was clearly a personal rebuke to him. It made him more determined to save the pine and thus the bottleneck in the street remained.

Neither side would give way. The Andalucistas were accused of blocking progress; the Centristas were said to be spending public money unnecessarily. The tree wasn't a pine anyway and it was probably riddled with dry rot; the tree was the only one in the street and an inspiration to all. But one morning the inspiration was gone. Overnight somebody had crept out and chopped the tree down.

It didn't make any difference. The council went ahead and bulldozed a piece of the house opposite, anyway. So both sides won. It was the closest the *pueblo* could get to what you could call a compromise.

Eusebio gave his verdict: "What this country needs is a 28-year-old Franco."

22

NO PASA NADA

A shriek of pain echoed down the Street of Bitterness, followed by a torrent of abusive language. Rushing to the door, I peered cautiously out. My God, there was blood on the cobbles. What the devil was happening? A revolution? The *bandoleros* had come back?

No, it turned out to be something more frightening. Caridad had declared war on Teresa and was pursuing her down the street with a fire tongs.

"I'm going for the Guardia. You'll not get away with this," sobbed Teresa, as she tried to staunch the blood from a head wound.

"Go on then!" yelled Caridad defiantly, waving the tongs. "See if I care. But next time you touch a hair of my son's head, I'll do more than give you a scratch, daughter of a whore!"

Teresa did go to the Civil Guard and some time later the two women were summoned to a local court where Caridad was fined 500 pesetas. It was not the first time. Caridad, petite, pretty and all flashing steel, was a volcano waiting to explode. There were other volcanoes around, I came to discover, in this so peaceful *pueblo*.

At first glance, it seemed the sort of place where nothing ever happened. As you approached from the coast (where almost anything could happen—and did), you sensed immediately that here was a community breathing solidarity and harmony. Here, you knew, you would find the rustic simplicity, down-to-earth values, and generosity of spirit that had vanished in the soulless cities. Here, so little happened that—

and I did not know whether to feel concerned or smug about the prospect—life might even end up being a trifle monotonous.

The villagers did their best to confirm this impression. They all agreed that it was a tranquil spot and they would frequently inform you of this. When I had been away for a few weeks, I would consult Miguel, my neighbour, about the latest news. He would shrug his shoulders.

"Here we are. *Un pueblo tranquilo.*"

"No news then?"

"It almost rained once, but in the end it didn't want to. Just two drops. That's all. *Aqui no pasa nada.* Nothing happens here."

At first I took his words at face value. However, after seeing Caridad in action, I began to wonder. Soon, Thea plugged into the village grapevine and we were learning about Mario's dawn dash through town with no clothes on, about the fight at the *fiesta*, the scandal at the town hall, and the near-riot in the plaza. Then there was the vampire scare. One night a youth was returning home late when a figure leaped from the shadows and bit deep into his shoulder. For a while everybody walked sideways in case the mystery attacker struck again.

One morning they came and took sad-eyed Jorge away from his home in the Street of Bitterness. His mother was removed later, in a coffin. Apparently, Jorge, growing tired of his mother's threats to return him to the asylum, had seized her by the throat and smashed her head against the wall until she could threaten him no more.

They found a goatherd one morning suspended from an olive tree on one of the terraced fields below the *pueblo*. They said that was the way it usually happened—when they took the final plunge, suicides wanted their last sight to be that of the *pueblo*. The suicides . . . they were the biggest shock. Cries of despair amid so much natural beauty.

There was more to the *pueblo* than the casual visitor could ever imagine. What *aqui no pasa nada* really meant, I came to understand, was "so many things have happened that it would take too long to tell you all about them."

The women endlessly gossiping in the streets and in the shops were not just chattering, as I had innocently believed, about the price of fish or the dress they had bought for the *feria*. They had meatier stuff to occupy their imaginations, as we realised when the real news began to filter through to us. It was the sort of stuff that had inspired García Lorca to write such dramatic plays as "Blood Wedding" and "The House of Bernardo Alba." Close to the tranquil surface there were seething passions, jealousy and envy, unreasoned hate and justified bitterness, frustration and desperation, which now and again exploded into the open like bubbles bursting in a cauldron. A typical rural community, you might say.

Land was at the root of violent quarrels that split entire families. Brother did not speak to brother, sister to sister because one felt the other had done them out of their rightful inheritance. As there were no large land-owners in the village, the piece of land involved could be just a miserable stretch of *secano*, unirrigated mountainside, or a *bancal*, a few square metres of rocky terrace. But the feuds went on for years.

When Jesusa down the street separated from Ignacio because of his drunken ways, she tried to make a separate life for herself. He went to live with his mother, but he could not accept this separation. It was a blow to his status, to his macho image, to his pride. But most of all it was a threat to his hopes to acquire a plot of land inherited by Jesusa. It became his obsession. She was married to him so what was hers was his, she was denying him his rights, it was her duty as a wife. Again and again, he demanded that she signed over the land to him, but in vain. Jesusa suspected that Ignacio wanted only to sell the land to raise some cash to feed his drinking habit.

One night the street was awakened by Jesusa's screams. Rejected once more by his wife, Ignacio had lost all reason. In a drunken rage, he had picked up Jesusa's sewing scissors and stabbed her 30 times. Fortunately, Jesusa survived. They took Ignacio away and we did not see him for some time. When he returned from jail, he was a changed and chastened man. He gave up drink and led a comparatively blameless life.

If arguments over land could provoke open war, losing face could lead to violence, as Joaquin discovered. Living dangerously was a way of life to Joaquin. He was a professional whitewasher, possessed of amazing energy and perpetual good humour. Scorning all safety precautions, he would clamber about the highest building, briskly slapping on whitewash and ignoring the cries of the spattered passers-by below. To watch his high-speed performance on the church was a little like witnessing a Keystone Cops film. He used a brush attached to a long bamboo pole. In dizzying succession, as he thrust his brush into the most inaccessible corners, he would shin up shaky scaffolding, dance across the roof, lean out from upper balconies, hang by his fingernails from the tower.

He always had a cheeky grin on his face, even when he fell off, which was not infrequent. On one occasion he tumbled three storeys, bouncing off a terrace into a patio. Picking himself up, he chuckled: "*Hierba mala nunca muere* (You can't kill a bad weed)" and walked away. The housewife who saw the incident fared worse. She fainted and was carried off to the doctor to receive sedatives for shock.

Joaquin was normally so speckled with whitewash that it was difficult to recognise him. It was only when I met him on a feast day, all spruced up and out with the family, that I realised he was not a white-haired 50-year-old but a dark-haired young fellow in his 30s. But then came an incident that threaded grey through his hair almost overnight.

Joaquin was fearless, but he made the mistake of publicly shaming a neighbour with whom he had a long-standing feud. The pet kitten belonging to Joaquin's daughter was the spark in the powderkeg. The neighbour complained that it was destroying his plants and trespassing in his house. If it happened once more, he would kill it. Joaquin came home one day to find the cat's body strung up outside his house. Infuriated, he stormed on to a building site where his enemy was working and launched a broadside of insults.

"Never, never do anything like that again or you will regret it," he cried. His harsh words voiced before others were taken as a public

affront, a blow to family pride. His neighbour's family was one with *mala leche*, as the saying went. You did not trifle with them for they carried their grudges from generation to generation.

A few days later, Joaquin went out to his vineyard to clear the weeds. In the heat of the afternoon, he went into the farmhouse and lay down for a snooze. Fortunately, as it turned out, he lay face down. He was awakened by a sharp pain in his neck. Standing over him was his neighbour, eyes bloodshot with alcohol and rage over the humiliation of the recent argument. He held a blood-stained sickle in his hand.

Blood spouting from a deep neck wound, Joaquin staggered to the next farmhouse to seek help. He arrived at the hospital near death, but he survived. Eventually he returned to work and there was the same cheerful smile on his lips as before, the same cheeky remark for all those he met. "*Hierba mala nunca muere*," he repeated, with his usual laugh. But he was not laughing inside. His attacker, released after questioning by the police, was still around. They crossed one another's paths every day, and you wondered when the hatred would erupt again.

While there was plenty of passion about, everyday crime was almost non-existent in the *pueblo*. This was partly because it was so difficult to get away with it in a society where everybody knew everybody else's business. It was impossible to keep a secret, let alone commit a theft, even out in the countryside. If you took so much as a tomato, you could be sure that somebody would see you.

When a crime did occur, it was of the typical rustic variety, as in the case of Rodrigo's hidden hoard. Rodrigo lived alone at the upper edge of the village, where his only neighbours were goats and mules. He was an ancient gnome of a man with a head like a half-inflated football, leathery and deeply wrinkled. He would sit on his doorstep and nod at you as you passed, but he spent a good part of his time muttering. He did this as he wandered the mule-tracks and he did it as he counted his money, which was frequently.

One morning, loud groans drew the neighbours to Rodrigo's hovel. They found him bloody and half-conscious. Two attackers had indulged in match practice with his head, it appeared. His life savings were gone.

It was the biggest case the *pueblo's* Civil Guard detachment had known in years. In Franco's era, when the mere sight of a tricorn hat was enough to strike a chill into many a local heart, this paramilitary force's chief task had been to watch for subversion. In their bleak barracks, where four or five guards lived with their families, they kept files on everybody and carefully documented the movements of any strangers. Segregated from village life, they seemed more of an occupying army than a police force, a reminder of the post-Civil War guerrilla conflict here. You would come on a patrol suddenly, in some remote spot in the countryside or as you returned to the village at midnight. The grim silhouette against a dim street lamp of two tricorned figures cradling submachine-guns was a potent inducement not to tangle with the law.

But the coming of democracy reduced police powers and fear of authority diminished. Crime began to rise across Spain. But our *pueblo* was sadly backward in such matters and you could still leave your door unlocked. The Civil Guards were somewhat underemployed, until the attack on Rodrigo occurred.

At last, they had a worthy challenge and they sprang into action. A few inquiries revealed that the previous night two men had been playing cards in one of the bars and losing heavily. Eventually, their cash exhausted, they left the bar. Half an hour later they returned, ordered drinks all round and began gambling again. To La Benemérita (the meritorious, as newspapers sometimes referred to the Guards with no hint of irony), this sounded like distinctly suspicious behaviour. The two men were invited to the barracks for a heart-to-heart talk in traditional Benemérita style. At first, the two said they had been so drunk they could remember little. Soon enough, however, their memories returned. It was conceivable, they admitted, that they had wrapped mule blankets around their heads to conceal their identities and beaten up Rodrigo until he revealed where he kept his money.

The culprits went to jail, but poor old Rodrigo recovered only part of his savings. Although he continued to mutter in his accustomed fashion, he was never quite the same again.

The case of The Phantom, of course, was in another league. One day I told the neighbours' children that I was about to walk up to the Castillo. They gaped at me in horror.

"Don't go! Not up there! The Phantom will get you."

It turned out that the mere mention of that name was sending delicious shivers through the *pueblo*. The affair had started with a young American girl. Taking a walk through the countryside one day, she paused to admire the wild flowers and the sheer tranquillity. When she raised her eyes, she found her path blocked by a figure with a knife in his hand. She was white-faced and incoherent when she stumbled back into the *pueblo*.

"It was weird, weird. No, I couldn't recognise him again. I couldn't see him properly—he had something over his face. He just pointed the knife at me and shouted awful things."

She abruptly cut short her stay, leaving the *pueblo* next day. Soon there was another incident. A young girl was returning from the family cortijo when a masked man leaped up before her and waved a knife under her nose. It happened again, and again. Any girl using one of the lonelier paths was likely to encounter the mysterious attacker, brandishing his knife. The Phantom, as he came to be known, was on the loose.

Although his main target was teenage girls, The Phantom apparently did not molest them. In fact, he seemed an easygoing sort of menace. He demanded money. If they did not have any, he could be bought off with sweets or a packet of sunflower seeds. The "awful things" the American girl had heard may well have been a misunderstanding; perhaps he was just asking for chewing gum. Despite this less than sinister aspect, however, the Phantom in his grotesque Carnival mask provoked real terror.

They got him in the end. He was caught and locked up in the town hall under heavy guard. A prison van drove up and he was shuffled into it escorted by Civil Guards. What a letdown it was. The dreaded Phantom proved to be a spotty youth with serious problems of adjustment, particularly with regard to the female sex. His humiliation was total, for the whole *pueblo* turned out to witness his departure.

The next day Miguel was walking down the street and I greeted him.

"*Qué tal,* Miguel? What's going on?"

"*Hombre,* here we are, as always. *No pasa nada.*" He yawned. "That's how it is in the *pueblo*."

23

WAR IN THE SIERRAS

On a grey and rainy morning in May, briefly, unwillingly, the *pueblo* focussed the attention of all Spain. Chauffeur-driven limousines toiled up the winding road and clogged the streets in search of parking places. Dignitaries in braid and ribbons and purple robes and dark suits alighted and stumbled about on the wet cobbles. Generals, the civil governor's representative, members of parliament, local mayors, the bishop, soldiers, television cameramen, reporters and photographers looked around uncertainly at this place most had surely never heard of until a few hours earlier.

It was a funeral that brought them to the village. All night in the parish church a guard of honour had stood over the coffin, draped with the national flag, as the villagers came to pay their respects. Everybody who could walk attended the service, those who could not squeeze into the church overflowing into the plaza. Tears ran down the cheeks of young and old as the priest intoned his funeral oration.

"Once again the blood has been spilt of a good man, who had to abandon his native village -like so many Andalusians-in order to gain his daily bread honourably," declared Paco El Cura. Paco could never resist injecting a political message and his words fell like a recrimination on the assembled dignitaries, who pursed their lips and bowed their heads. "We must condemn all violence since it is the gravest attempt against human dignity... "

Living in the *pueblo* it was easy to forget the harsh world outside, but the death of Antonio was a reminder that we could not stay untouched by events in the rest of Spain. He had been an upright young fellow, a member of the Royal Guard and the pride of his family. Up there in Madrid he drove the top brass about. Imagine it, *un chico del pueblo* (a village boy) with an important position in the capital.

Then one morning, when he halted at a traffic light, a motorcyclist drew up alongside. The pillion passenger dropped a plastic bag on the roof of the car and the motorcycle took off at high speed. Seconds later, the bomb blasted through the car roof, killing Antonio, a lieutenant-colonel and another soldier.

ETA, the terrorist organisation demanding independence for the Basque Country, was responsible. They could justify the killings in a hundred ways, as such movements always do. All was legitimate in the battle against the oppressors of Madrid. Anybody who wore uniform was a member of the army of occupation and therefore a valid target. When you were fighting for freedom, spilling blood was sometimes necessary. Even when a few tourists or children got in the way. ETA would shrug. Mistakes could happen, but the end justifies the means.

Antonio was one of hundreds who had died in the brutal, senseless conflict. The funerals often took place in poor villages of Extremadura and Andalusia, for it was from these that came many of the recruits for the Civil Guard, the army, and the police. Enlistment offered an escape from the hardships of rural life and the guarantee of food and shelter, even the education their parents had been unable to give them. The people of those *pueblos* understood nothing of the Basque cause. They saw only the results of their independence campaign, when the bodies came home.

As the coffin was borne from the church by six of Antonio's comrades, the crowd broke into applause and there were cries of "*Viva España*", "Long live the Army!" and "ETA murderers!". Then there was only the shuffling of feet as the funeral cortege made its way along the main street. Sheets with black crepe pinned to them hung from the house balconies. In a thin drizzle, the procession laboured up the steps to the cemetery, which stood on a hillside, the cypresses rising like sentinels above its white walls.

Inside, there were grief-stricken scenes as the casket was eased into its niche and the cemetery official stirred up the cement he had prepared, then methodically bricked up the tomb. Outside, something occurred which heightened the underlying tension. A dozen or so youths suddenly thrust up their arms in the Fascist salute and sang *Cara al Sol,* the old Falange song. There were angry mutterings from the mourners and one of the soldiers remonstrated with the group, most of them were not from the *pueblo.*

"What do they think they're doing?" protested the villagers. "This is not the time for that sort of performance."

It only needed an incident of that sort to create uneasiness, for bitter memories lurked just below the deceptively tranquil surface. There were things that the villagers preferred not to talk about, they were too painful, but they could not forget. When somebody broke into the cemetery chapel one night and defiled a religious image, a shudder of alarm went through the older folk, who recalled how the church had been vandalised in the Civil War. They were only reassured when it emerged that it was not the *Rojos* on the rampage again but a couple of juvenile delinquents.

Franco, the implacable Generalísimo who had conducted a personal crusade for more than 40 years, may have been interred in the Valley of the Fallen, but his ghost was still abroad. A few months earlier a bunch of Civil Guards had stormed parliament in Madrid and held the nation's elected government at gunpoint for 18 hours. They planned to save Spain from godlessness and the Reds and turn the clock back to 1936. The bungled conspiracy proved to be one of the last gasps of Francoism, but the *pueblo* was not to know that and the rightwing choir outside the cemetery clearly did not want to know.

The incident, in fact, was especially provocative, because it recalled another incident at the cemetery, when anti-Franco guerrillas (or "people of the sierra" as they were popularly known) were locked in a struggle with the Nationalist forces. Civil War memories were comparatively fresh among the villagers, because the conflict had not ended when the Nationalists marched triumphantly into Madrid and Barcelona in 1939 but a dozen years later.

In the 1940s a guerrilla war had raged in Southern Spain, a war I had never heard of until I came to the *pueblo*. Although in my English school we learned a good deal about the Spaniards and their Invincible Armada, for some reason the peninsula's recent history barely rated a mention. The guerrilla conflict had been a nasty, brutal affair that dragged on for years, but was hardly reported inside or outside the country.

Some of the *gente de la sierra* were men who had broken the law and in the time-honoured way of Andalusia had taken to the hills. Others were merely politically suspect. After the Civil War, a member of the Socialist party or a trade union official had few choices; he could flee the country or go into hiding. He could also throw himself on the mercy of the regime, but there were serious doubts about receiving any merciful treatment. When Nationalist troops had stormed into the *pueblo* early in the Civil War, the leading leftists had already made their getaway. So the vengeful rebels arrested eight Republican sympathisers, including the mayor. Weeping women hurled themselves before the wheels of the vehicles carrying away the detainees, but it made no difference. After a speedy court-martial, they were executed.

In the mid-1940s, matters became serious when hard-line Communists, determined to topple Franco and his hated regime, organised the fugitives in the mountains into a full-scale guerrilla movement. Arms and men were ferried across the Mediterranean from Algeria and slipped ashore under cover of darkness in one of the coves not far from the *pueblo*.

A ruthless commander known as Roberto set about creating a highly-disciplined force, entrenched in the craggy, uninhabited ranges behind the village. At one time he is said to have controlled up to 150 men and he kept them in line with exemplary punishments; malcontents or suspected informers were strangled with nooses of esparto cord. Of all the rebel groups operating across Spain, that led by Roberto proved to be one of the most troublesome to the authorities. They raised cash by holdups, extortion and kidnappings. Those suspected of passing information to the Civil Guard could expect no mercy. To be labelled a *chivato* (squealer) was a sentence of death. Inevitably, some used the situation to settle old accounts by wrongfully accusing neighbours against whom they had a grudge.

Hundreds of soldiers, Civil Guards, and Regulares (Moorish troops with a fearsome reputation) were sent to the area to hunt down the *bandoleros* (bandits) as the regime termed them. A curfew was imposed on the village and patrols on foot and horseback combed the sierras. Franco's men took few prisoners and inflicted horrendous torture on those who were taken in an effort to extract information from them. One of my neighbours pointed out a former Civil Guard sergeant, sleek and paunchy in his middle age, who had retired to live in a neighbouring town.

"He was the worst, for he not only tortured but took pleasure in it. He married a local girl, but to this day he does not dare walk through the *pueblo*."

Caught between two fires, the villagers feared both sides. By night the rebels would creep down from the mountains and seek food from the farmhouses. If villagers did not cooperate, they could expect reprisals. If they did, they faced the wrath of the authorities. To stop food being smuggled to the guerrillas, farmers were checked when they went out to the fields every morning. Anybody carrying more food than necessary for his own needs could expect a fierce interrogation. It was a time when nobody felt safe, for almost every family had a relative involved in the struggle, on one side or the other. Some villagers spent time in gaol, others lost husbands or fathers, sometimes through betrayal by their neighbours.

There were too many funerals in those days. But one in particular stuck in the memory of Antonio, the village historian. The incident at the cemetery prompted him to recall another grim day when the people of the *pueblo* had marched up that same hillside.

Although his schooling had been limited, as Antonio's hair turned to silver he acquired a definite academic air. His house bulged with bound volumes and artefacts he had picked up in his field work, Moorish bones, fragments of weapons, a Phoenician pot, traces of the waves of invaders who had passed this way. He had burrowed through countless dusty archives and yellowing documents in search of any mention of our *pueblo* and its place in Spanish history. He was writing a book about it, several books. They might never be finished, but that was hardly important. It was the hunt that mattered, tracking down the details, making new discoveries.

However, Antonio did not need to look through his books to recall his teenage years when the rebels were in the sierras.

"They were terrible times," he told me. "But one day in particular will always stay in my memory. It was extraordinary, emotional. It started when the Maquis discovered that one of the villagers, El Moreno, was acting as a double agent, passing information to both

sides. They gave him a choice—die or join us. But to prove that he was really with them he had to kill one of the opposition forces. El Moreno, in fear of his life, I suppose, agreed. When he came across a Moorish soldier on his knees making obeisance to Mecca, he crept up on him and smashed his head open with an axe. Then he fled to the sierra with another youth."

"They sent a new man from Madrid to take command here, a Captain Fernández. He was dying of cancer, that man, and he was ruthless and without pity. He went into action and arrested three youths whose relations were in the sierra. Then he sent a message to the rebels that the boys would die unless El Moreno was handed over. At that time the Civil Guard made use of something called the *ley de fugas*. It meant that anybody could be shot on the grounds that they were trying to escape."

"Well, the guerrillas ignored the ultimatum and Fernández had the three shot. I remember it was a strange day, a cool Sunday in April, 1950, and there was an odd yellowish tinge to the light. I had been to church and when I came out, one of the villagers, a half-crazy fellow, was coming down the street, crying 'They've killed them, they've killed them!' The whole village went into a state of shock. They just could not believe it. The bodies were taken to the cemetery, but Captain Fernández refused to allow a proper funeral service in the church."

"That was too much for the *pueblo*. Domingo the priest told everybody to come to the church that evening when the bells started tolling. The whole village turned up and Domingo said mass. Then the men lifted up the coffins and carried them through the streets. Everybody was there, the mayor, the doctor, the councillors, 2000 people walking behind the coffins in silence. A silence you would not believe, with just the bell tolling, and the young Civil Guards looking on, fingering their weapons, nervous, white-faced, not knowing what to do. The tension was tremendous. The cortege climbed up to the cemetery and the three were given Christian burial. And then the people went home in orderly fashion, before the curfew."

"Captain Fernández was crazy with anger. The next day he called the leading members of the community to his headquarters and launched a tirade of insults. He called them *hijos de putas*, anti-patriots, traitors, and he and his men gave them a vicious beating. But Domingo the priest was not with them. He hadn't stayed in the village. Instead, he had slipped out and headed for safety in Málaga."

In the end, Roberto was arrested in Madrid and allegedly gave away all his fellow guerrillas. The last of the rebels were "shot while escaping" or court martialled and executed or jailed. The guerrilla movement was wiped out. Some escaped by the skin of their teeth and by sheer chance. In one of the remotest villages in the sierras, I came across Manolo el Rubio, once one of the most hunted men in Spain in the 1940s when he led a guerrilla group. A case of mistaken identity spared him from summary justice.

"When the Guardia killed six comrades in an ambush in 1949, they thought I was one of the dead," growled Manolo. "So they stopped looking for me. There was no way of escape, so I went into hiding and waited for Franco to die."

For 27 years he hid out on a remote farm, convinced that the death penalty awaited him if he were discovered. His faithful female companion smuggled him food and he passed his time listening to the radio, emerging for a little exercise only at night. Finally, just after Franco died, his existence was discovered. Manolo was the last of the Civil War *topos*— or moles as they were known—to reveal themselves. The charges against him were shelved.

When I asked him if he still believed in the revolution, he replied: "I have always believed in the revolution." He was a man carved from granite, tough, unyielding, unrepentant. Ana, the woman who had guarded his secret for so many years, was just as resilient. When Manolo emerged from hiding, the couple were married.

Those harsh and hungry times had left a permanent mark on our *pueblo*. Some villagers had served jail terms. Many had fled to the factories of Barcelona or emigrated to Argentina, where they congregated in a rural community, trying to recreate the life they had left behind. Often those who went were the brightest and most adventurous. The *pueblo* had had the stuffing knocked out of it and it took decades to recover.

In Barcelona I came across the village's last surviving *guerrillero*, a shadow of a man who as a teenager had joined the band in the mountains only to encounter brutal disillusionment. El Caniyo (The Reed), told me: "We were just illiterate village boys who knew nothing. Life was hard and the people of the sierra lured us with talk of regular pay. The chiefs talked about liberating Spain from Franco, but I didn't even know who Franco was. We slept on the ground amid the pines with just a jacket for shelter. I never fired a shot in anger. I had to fetch water, that's all. Slaves, that's what we were. I realised I'd been fooled.

"You couldn't trust anybody. The chiefs watched us all the time in case we tried to desert. They couldn't let you leave for fear you would give information to the Civil Guard. If somebody was said to have been sent to the Sierra Nevada, you knew you probably wouldn't see him again. I was scared for my life. In the end I ran away, walking, walking over the mountains until I got back to the village. Then, as I knew they would hunt me down, I joined the Legion and was sent to North Africa. And there I finally learned to read and write."

El Duende (the goblin) was another of the *gente de la sierra* who had survived. He had been a *contrabandista* (smuggler) and had aided the landing of guerrillas on the coast. Small, shrivelled but still pugnacious, he could not hide his contempt for Fascism, whether Franco was alive or dead. If there was any reference to the Nationalists on television while he was in a bar, he would snap: "Nonsense! What a load of crap!" and similar comments. Any Civil Guards present discreetly lowered their heads and pretended not to hear.

El Duende it was who first introduced us to the *pueblo*, before we had bought a house. He guided us around the bars during January's San Sebastian *fiesta*, greeting old friends and consuming the local wine. Well-oiled, he talked of his life, of fighting with the Republicans against the Nationalist rebels, then years as a guerrilla, then more years in prison after he was caught. Late in the evening, he suddenly ripped open his shirt to reveal his belly. It was a remarkable sight. El Duende was lean, but his belly was large, protruding and shaped like a shoebox with rounded edges. A livid, foot-long scar, like a sabre cut, ran vertically down this unappetising spectacle.

"Look at that!" said El Duende proudly.

"*Madre mía*! How did you get it? In the war?"

He shook his head scornfully.

"In the sierras?"

"Hah!"

"All right, in prison?"

"No, no, no."

He chuckled, a chuckle tempered by years of hard living and *aguardiente* breakfasts.

"In hospital, *por Dios*! Appendicitis! Appendicitis!"

El Duende was amusing company, as long as you were on his side. Only later did I learn why he was held in awe. It was rumoured that during his time in the sierras, after despatching an enemy, he always sliced off the ears to keep as a trophy.

24

A POWERFUL GENTLEMAN

It did not signify much by itself, but the day I went to the *estanco* and they didn't wrap my postage stamps I knew that an era had ended. They had always wrapped the postage stamps, you understand. Even if you had only spent three pesetas, which used to be enough to deliver your letter to Madrid, Julio or his wife always laid the stamp on a piece of paper, carefully folded over the two sides, and tucked in the edges, before handing it you. The little exercise was performed, if not exactly ceremoniously, with a certain style. Then, one day, they stopped doing it.

It was an indication of significant changes taking place in the *pueblo*. Old customs were dying out. New ways were taking over. Carmencita's grocery store was no longer a treasure house of mysterious boxes and sacks, into which she would delve to dig out beans and flour and other foodstuffs. Everything came glossily pre-packaged these days. A supermarket had opened, a supermarket in the *pueblo*! Television aerials sprouted from every house, the first satellite dish appeared. Paco, Miguel, and Sebastian had sold their mules and bought cars. Their sons were clamouring for motor-cycles. Who could spare the time and effort to gift wrap such a paltry item as a stamp? People had better things to do. There were new priorities. There was money to be made.

It was a slow process, but the *pueblo* was being infected by the fever that had gripped the coast and turned the way of life down there inside out. You could see its effect on the nearest town, which had been the *pueblo's* poor relation. Down there, until recently, nobody had ever had a bean. Unlike the *pueblo*, where each family had its own intensely cultivated terrace, few of the townsfolk possessed any land. Some rented fields from the wealthy Larios family. The Marques de Larios and his heirs ruled the coast in feudal style, what with their sugar mills, distilleries, fine houses and countless acres of farmland from Marbella to Motril.

When we first came to the coast, apart from spots like Torremolinos and Marbella where tourism was taking off, little had changed since a poetic youth named Laurie Lee passed that way in the 1930s and noted the "salt-fish villages, thin-ribbed, sea-hating." In the nearest coastal town to the *pueblo*, the inhabitants lived, or rather managed to survive, from fishing and cultivating potatoes, tomatoes, sweet potatoes, and sugar cane. Those who had no land at all, the *jornaleros* (day labourers), used to stand every morning outside one of the bars, waiting to be contracted. For all their proudly independent air, the fishermen were no better off. They lived in hovels near the beaches and, since the in-shore waters were fished out, their efforts brought them little reward.

"They were as poor as church mice," said the villagers contemptuously. They looked down in more than one sense on their neighbours. "Why, they were so poor they used to come up here begging. You could never put much trust in them. They're not *gente seria* (reliable people) down there on the coast, not like the people of the sierras."

These days, however, envy lurked behind their comments, for the tables had been turned. The paupers on the coast had acquired wealth and all its trappings with bewildering speed. Tourists had begun flocking in and the poverty-stricken settlement had grown into a resort. On the main beach where fishermen had dozed in the shade of their boats, once accessible only along a precipitous path, apartments, shops, snack bars and restaurants now lined the sands. Ploughmen had become cooks and waiters, fishing families sold souvenirs, shopkeepers became supermarket tycoons, former bricklayers ruled construction empires. And useless pieces of rocky terrain had been transmuted into gold.

The *pueblo* looked on in amazement and chagrin. The gold rush was passing them by, just because of a sheer accident of geography, just because those church mice had a beach. The villagers tried to maintain a dignified aloofness, but they could not help being affected by the tourist invasion. There were well-paid jobs in construction for a start, as villas and apartment blocks started sprouting up. And there were all those pliable foreign girls looking for Latin lovers.

Until then the only source of sexual relief for lusty males had been a visit to the sleazy *puticlubs*, the garishly-lit whore houses located on the fringes of the coastal towns. Now their business dropped sharply. Village Romeos came back with remarkable stories. The *suecas*, (the Swedes) as all the blonde invaders were known at first, were crazy for it. You did not even have to promise to marry them. They would do it the first night, just like that. The village girls, taught the virtues of chastity from birth, could not compete.

"I don't see my boyfriend all summer because he is down on the coast every night," sighed Conchie, demurely embroidering table-cloths for the wedding day in five years' time. But she was resigned to the situation. It was one more cross a woman had to bear. "I know he'll be back in October. He may chase those shameless blondes, but it's me he's going to marry."

Even so, the village girls began to change their ways. The more daring ones started going out with their *novios* unchaperoned. Soon they were not just holding hands in public, but even kissing. Soon they were wearing sexy fashions and dancing the nights away in the village disco. The new morality took the *pueblo* by storm. It was hardly surprising that the old-timers wandered about with dazed expressions on their faces. In Franco's time everything had been forbidden. Now anything was possible.

Even nudity. Not so long ago, no respectable female ventured into the street with her arms uncovered. She would certainly never be seen in a swimsuit. In fact, despite the closeness of the sea, the villagers rarely visited the beach. It was not the custom. Then the sexual revolution arrived. Rumours circulated that Guillermo's daughter had been seen topless on the beach, then it was Francisca's daughter.

"It's becoming like Sweden, total depravity. Democracy is turning us into the arsehole of Europe," mourned Eusebio, adding: "Franco would never have allowed this." But, when a German made him a juicy offer for a stony hillside, he did not hesitate to benefit from the winds of change. Some of the gold that had swamped the coast was creeping up the valley to the *pueblo*, turning values on their heads.

"*Yo cago en Dios*! I shit on God!" muttered Miguel, unable to disguise his bitterness. "You work your guts out improving your farm, fertilising and irrigating, until you've got the fattest tomatoes and biggest potatoes. And suddenly my neighbour, who never did anything except run a few goats over a bit of wasteland, becomes a millionaire. Just because his miserable plot has a view of the sea. What's the good of that when there's no water? Those foreigners are crazy."

Stories of peasant guile and tourist gullibility were legion. Some were even true. Pepe moved to the coast to trawl for prospects and was always gloating over how he had hooked another fish.

"I tell them I have inherited some land but I have to sell it to pay for my children's education. That always appeals."

Pepe would take his sun-dazzled victims to a hillside plot with a magnificent view. Just by chance, an old man would come riding along on a donkey. He was a charming type with a wide smile, who would bid the clients welcome and gallantly offer them the fruit of his fields, a bunch of grapes, a kilo of oranges. Then, with a courteous sweep of his straw hat, he would ride off into the sunset.

"What a gracious old fellow!" said the clients, bowled over by the sheer picturesqueness of the whole scene.

"He'll be your neighbour. Isn't he a dear old chap?" said Pepe, steering them towards his office and the signing of a worthless sales contract.

After they had paid their deposit, they often went back to the site of their future villa to enjoy the scene and dream a little. The dream was shattered by the arrival of a new character in the charade, who angrily demanded what they were doing on his land and abruptly turfed them off. They never found Pepe again. He lay low until they flew home, then looked for the next prospect. He sold the same plot of land over and over again, living quite well off the deposits he collected.

"It's black money. They're all dodging taxes in their own countries," he said with glib certainty. "They won't dare to stir up a fuss."

When a successful artist bought a building plot far out in the country, he thought he had found the ideal place to follow his muse, far from other dwellings and worldly considerations. He built a magnificent studio. Then, one day amiable old Lázaro, who had sold him the plot, casually mentioned that the piece of land alongside was also available.

"I don't need any more land, thanks," said the painter.

"Ah, well, I just wanted you to have the first chance. It's a fine site for a house and I'm sure it will fetch a good price. One or two folk have already inquired," said Lázaro.

"You can't be serious. The house would be right next to my studio."

"Reckon it would be a bit of company for you."

"But the only reason I bought here was to be away from everybody!"

Not-so-amiable-any-more Lázaro shrugged his shoulders.

"That land has no irrigation. It's just vines and, you know, you can't make a living from them. If I get a good offer for the land, I have to sell. Of course, if you want it yourself, we could come to some arrangement."

They came to an "arrangement," a costly one. Lots of other purchases were being "arranged." In the *pueblo* it suddenly seemed that everybody had a house for sale. They would edge up to me and suggest that if I could find a buyer there would be something in it for me. Prices shot skywards, particularly after word spread that an Englishman had bought a stable for the equivalent of the town hall

annual budget. Asking prices were calculated with little reference to the actual value of the property. They depended on how much was wanted by each relative participating in the windfall; the going rate was soon one million pesetas per person. This led to long and sometimes painful negotiations. It was best to deal with small families.

Even then complications could arise. Many houses had no title deeds. Tattered bits of paper bearing indecipherable information quilled last century would be dredged up, but that was all. In the past, nobody had ever bothered to register changes of ownership. There was no need to when the *pueblo* was a tight-knit community that few outsiders ever penetrated. It was clear enough which family owned what and, in addition, officially registered sales attracted taxes. Nobody wanted to pay those.

Other problems could arise too, as Rafaela explained to a buyer of her windowless cave.

"Very well, you can have the house. But remember. That room is Uncle Carlos's."

"Uncle Carlos?"

"Yes, he went to France in 1960. He's never been back. But, if he does return, remember the room is his. My mother gave it him."

The 10-percenters were not slow to arrive. Since few of the buyers could speak a word of Spanish and nobody in the *pueblo* had mastered a foreign tongue, the situation was ideal for middlemen to make a killing. Neither side knew what the other was saying. Only the middleman was aware of what was really going on. Foreigners had a pathetic trust in their fellow-countrymen, a circumstance that the 10 percenters exploited to the full. Thus it was that Briton duped Briton, German conned German, and Danes diddled Danes.

El Habichuela (the runner-bean) was the master. A scrawny Scandinavian, he moved into the village with holes in his shoes and a sales patter in several languages. He set about hijacking possible clients, on buses, in bars and restaurants. Within a few months he was surprisingly affluent. To the naive newcomers, he appeared a guardian angel who would handle all their problems. He wore a permanent grin as he introduced them to property-owners, haggled over a purchase, took the cash from the buyer and handed at least some of it to the seller, organised building improvements and the purchase of furniture, helped with the paying of taxes and fees. You had no worries with El Habichuela. He was so obliging and always good-humoured, especially when he pocketed bundles of banknotes thrust upon him by eager clients. His smile never faltered.

Occasionally, much later, the buyers would uncover the truth. They had paid one price, the sellers had received another, and they had paid twice the going rate for building and furnishings, their new house had been built illegally, they received threatening letters from the building authorities. El Habichuela kept smiling, although if you looked more closely you saw that it was not really a smile at all. He just had protruding teeth.

El Habichuela made plenty of enemies in the *pueblo*, but it did not deter him. Nor did it deter the villagers from putting more business his way.

"*Hay que aprovechar*. You have to get the benefit," they said, bowled over by the value that flaking whitewash and rocky hillsides had suddenly acquired.

It really seemed that the village was taking off when signs started popping up like mushrooms announcing that the *pueblo* had become the "world's first *reserva biocultural*." Arrows indicated the location of a "*Ciudad Biointegrada*," an "*Espacio Agrobiológico*" and the "*Parque Biomático*." Nobody quite knew what all this inferred but soon a lone pine tree was planted on a barren hillside and a small hut constructed in its shade. This, it turned out, was the information office for a project that set half the village drooling in anticipation and the other half recoiling in alarm. We were privileged folk, it appeared. Investors were all set to spend colossal amounts of cash to create an ecological wonderland in our unique environment that would attract thousands of visitors and employ hundreds of locals. Just coincidentally, the so-called Green World also included plans for some "bio-climatic" dwellings or, to be more precise, for up to 4000 houses.

It was an amazing project in many ways, not least a plan to span a deep gorge with a suspension bridge. But it was also worrying; the prospect of sudden wealth split the village, provoking violent reactions. As the arguments grew fiercer, sceptics found it safer to hold their tongues. Blows were exchanged when they voiced their concerns. But you couldn't help wondering who were these big investors with millions to burn. Strangely enough, the companies named on the elaborate brochures didn't seem to figure in any official register. Environmentalists suggested that just possibly the "*reserva biocultural*" was a front for unrestrained development. And the regional authorities disclaimed any knowledge of the project. They pointed out that most of the wild sierra involved, the property of the *pueblo*'s largest land-owning family, was about to be declared a nature park, with tight controls on its use.

Then the town hall began to back-pedal. Nothing had actually been approved yet, said the mayor. In the information office on the hillside they kept handing out glossy brochures. But after a few months, very quietly, it closed its doors. The brightly painted signs began to peel and fade. The Green World's symbolic lone pine shrivelled and died. The "*Ciudad Biointegrada*" was stillborn.

Not that anybody seemed to learn any lessons from this debacle. "*Hay que aprovechar*," was a powerful argument. It was used by those who queued once a month outside the town hall to register for the *paro* (dole). In the past farm-workers had had no security blanket and often led a hand-to-mouth existence, but the Socialist government had remedied that, raining largesse on the poorer regions, including Andalusia, which happened to be one of their strongholds. Those in the dole queue, housewives, bricklayers, ploughmen, tile-layers, and others who had managed to spare a moment from more urgent business, had never had it so good.

One of the newly rich was Dionisio. He was in the bank one day, cashing the unemployment payment for his brother.

"You can't do this," said the clerk. "Your brother has to come in person and sign for this money himself."

"Don't be ridiculous," retorted Dionisio. "How can he find the time? He's at work."

It was a reasonable question. When a man is building houses, tilling his land at weekends, and running between his village home and coastal apartment, there is precious little time left to collect the dole. And, if he does not collect the dole, how the devil is he going to keep up the payments on his Nissan Patrol and video camera?

The villagers had a further argument to justify taking advantage of the situation, one learned in the lean years when potatoes and figs were the daily diet.

"*Poderoso caballero es Don Dinero*," they would say. And everybody would nod their heads and repeat the magic maxim. "It's true—a powerful gentleman is Mr. Money."

25

SPRITES AND WITCHES

At first sight, El Castillo was hardly impressive. In fact, as castles go, the *pueblo's* was a disappointment. El Castillo was a grandiose title for the half-buried traces of old walls which crowned a flat-topped hill above the village. By day it was a pleasant spot. In spring and early summer, the little plateau within the castle walls would be thick with grass and wild flowers and you might find a donkey calmly grazing there. It was a place to listen to the cicadas and contemplate the heavens. If you looked south, you could see the sea and an occasional glint from the traffic hurrying along the coast road. If you looked north, your gaze met a series of jagged peaks. Clouds dodged about them, forming and reforming. Wisps of moisture rising above the stern mountain barrier often swelled into what looked like flying saucers. Lulled by the hum of insects, you could spend hours watching those clouds as your thoughts wandered freely.

At sunset, the pattern of tiled roofs and whitewashed cubes of the village sprawled below was thrown into golden relief and the western sky became a canvas of brilliant colour. As scarlet melted into purple and deep black, a breeze would spring up and quite swiftly the atmosphere about the Castillo changed.

If you were alone up there, you could sense a chill even on a summer evening, and it did not require too much imagination to sense that the bloody events of the past still haunted the spot. Moorish rebels had once made a desperate last stand against Castilian forces in and around the castle. When the attack began, they hurled rocks down on the invaders with terrible effect. When they were over-run, the survivors fled into the mountains, the womenfolk balancing children on their shoulders as they skipped from rock to rock. Thousands died that day, the castle was demolished, and the Moors expelled from the area. Skulls, spearheads, and sword fragments occasionally turned up on the hillsides above the village. And legends endured.

At one point inside the ramparts, the ground fell away into a round indentation several metres long. This, it was believed, had been the entrance to a secret escape route which led down through the rock to connect with the *pueblo*. The idea was not so far-fetched, as the country round about was honeycombed with caves, some extending considerable distances. There were tales of strong draughts of cold air issuing from crevices in the rock which formed the back wall of many houses.

According to one story, the tunnel emerged at a Moorish tower in the *pueblo*. Nobody ever found this exit, but one day Doña Madalena, who had converted the tower into a comfortable home, told me that odd things had happened. She was a newcomer to the village, a sophisticated, self-possessed lady who would have sent any half-baked phantom packing. Even so...

"I don't know what's going on," she told me. "Every evening, at the same time, my dogs become very nervous. They start bristling and growling for no apparent reason. And door locks have jammed inexplicably. Then last week I returned home to find water flooding the terrace. A stop-cock had been left open. I never touch it and the only possible access to the terrace is through a locked door. And only I have the key. It does make one wonder."

An English family whose house bounded one side of the tower also reported strange happenings.

"Several times I have awakened at four in the morning with an odd prickling sensation about my head and scalp," said the husband, a doctor accustomed to dispassionate analysis. "Then the bathroom light goes on by itself. I've tested that switch and it will not move of its own accord. The most unnerving experience was to awake once in the early hours and hear the sound of a tennis ball bouncing. I called out to my two young sons to see if they were playing tricks, but they were both asleep. Visitors have told of other occurrences, a waste-basket moving from one spot to another, doors slamming."

"But there's a good feeling about this house. I think we have a benign spirit here."

Other spirits floating about the *pueblo* were more mischievous. One family was known to harbour a poltergeist. At their farmhouse, the goats were loosed from their barn during the night, milk churns tossed over, chairs overturned. Later when they moved to a house on the Street of Bitterness, pictures fell from walls and objects on the mantelpiece took flight. Then, so it was said, a daughter married and moved away and the strange incidents immediately stopped.

But there were other, inexplicable things, especially after Martin died. He was a Hungarian leprechaun who had lost his way and his wife and alighted in the *pueblo*. Alone in his house, he would play mournful solos on his saxophone, emerging now and then to pursue schemes that would make his fortune but were always doomed to failure. He talked about large sums of money that he was owed, but he was always penniless. Outwardly, he seemed cheerful for he had the face of a sprite, but those rubbery features and rolling pop-eyes let him down. People could not take him seriously.

He would buttonhole you to relate anecdotes that were sometimes humorous, often malicious, increasingly fantasy. As he drank more, the stories and his eyes became wilder. People started to avoid him. Which made one feel guilty afterwards. Maybe if somebody had listened . . .

Martin would tug at his unwilling listener's arm and roll those eyes. A clown who was dying inside.

"They're out to kill me. I know too much. I could get them sent away, so they'll stop at nothing to shut me up. They're after me."

Was he joking? It was hard to tell. Was it the alcohol, drugs? Who were "they"?

One night there were loud noises in Martin's house, yells and the sound of furniture crashing over. One neighbour said later she

heard Martin crying for help, but she paid no attention. He had been drunk so many times. The next morning he was found in the patio below his terrace, his head smashed. He died in hospital.

I went to the funeral. Only a handful of people turned up for the ceremony. Six of the villagers carried the simple coffin up to the cemetery, where it was slid into one of the niches and sealed up with bricks and mortar. There were no relatives present. The body had lain in a morgue for weeks as messages were sent to Hungary to try to locate Martin's family, but nobody claimed him. At the end he had neither family nor friends, except the villagers. They paid for the funeral. They had never understood Martin, but for a while he had been one of them.

A year later I bumped into a newcomer to the village who had rented Martin's house.

"Did you know the fellow?" he asked me. "I feel I do because he is still around. The last tenants said so, too. They were so frightened they moved out. I don't believe in spirits and all that nonsense, but there is definitely a presence in this house. Nothing sinister, but some-body there. You feel he wants to make contact."

But this fellow was hardly a reliable witness. Shortly after-wards, he abruptly disappeared from the *pueblo*. At first I thought Martin's ghost had frightened him away, but no, it was something more mundane. He had simply done a moonlight flit. Although only in the *pueblo* a few weeks, he had managed to dupe a good part of the population, borrowing large sums from Spaniards and expatriates alike. The police hunted him up the coast, but he had vanished as completely as any spirit.

Josefa could probably have made contact with Martin, had she wanted to. She heard voices to which the rest of us were not privy. Unusually sallow-complexioned, small, lean and intense, she was the closest thing to a witch that I have encountered.

Josefa arrived on our doorstep late one night in a bedraggled and confused state. I had not seen her for a long while, but had heard that, after a long relationship, she and Felipe had split up and were not even talking. At first it was not clear why she had called. She looked feverishly about the room and talked about her need for "living space." Then, Felipe's name came up.

"I'm still in contact with him," she said.

"You still see him?" I asked, in surprise.

"We communicate," she said, enigmatically. I noticed how sallow her skin was, much darker than I remembered. She had a wild and unpredictable air, yet at the same time there was a smugness about her as though she knew something that the rest of us didn't.

"You mean you have talked to him recently?"

"We don't need to talk. I tell you we're in contact, all the time." She clutched my arm, her black eyes burning.

"People don't understand. I have been trying to paint but I need space, living space. How can I work if I don't have living space?"

She intoned the Spanish words *espacio vital* in a way that leant them an almost mystic significance. "*Espacio vital*," she had to have "*espacio vital*." It was close to midnight and Josefa made no move to leave. Finally, she asked if she could stay the night. There was something disturbing about Josefa and I was not sure that I wanted her in the same house. But, at that hour, it would have been boorish to refuse. The next morning she made no move to depart. She had nowhere else to go, she said.

"Can't I stay here? I need living space so that I can create."

Those eyes shone with odd intensity. Her hair was tangled and dirty and she gave off a strong odour. Although the bathroom was next door to her room, however, she showed no interest in taking a shower. She sat on the floor, strumming a guitar tunelessly. Her influence, somehow vaguely threatening, seemed to pervade the whole house.

I took a walk to the bar and casually mentioned her presence to a friend. He grabbed my arm in alarm.

"Staying in your place? Get her out or you'll never get rid of her," he said urgently. "She's bad news. She has no friends left and she drove away all Felipe's friends."

"Yes, but she needs help."

"Forget it. I tried to help her. Everybody has tried to help her. It's hopeless. She's real trouble." He paused. "There's something about her. I'm sure that woman is bewitched. I get a strange feeling around her. For example, the other day she appeared just as I was getting into my car and asked me to give her a lift. I refused because I want nothing more to do with her. Then I drove straight off to the next town and guess what? The first person I saw was Josefa, walking down the street towards me, with that smile on her face. I tell you, the hairs rose on the back of my neck."

Refusing to accept the break with Felipe, Josefa had been pursuing him obsessively. Her well-off family from a distant part of Spain had rented an apartment for her, but she preferred to sleep on Felipe's doorstep. Whenever he went out, she followed him. If he entered a bar or restaurant, she entered, sitting where she could observe all he did. If he caught a bus, she did too, never taking her eyes from him. It had been a source of humour at first, but soon Felipe's nerves were shattered. Eventually, in desperation, he had called the police. They had taken Josefa off for psychiatric examination, but no grounds could be found for detaining her and as soon as she was released she returned to Felipe's doorstep.

Apparently, she had landed on my doorstep after Felipe had given her the slip and fled the village. The next day I escorted Josefa to the nearest coastal town and suggested that she should go to her apartment there. When I wished her luck, she said nothing but looked at me with a strange smile about her lips.

Back home, before going to bed, I went around checking the doors. The back-door near which Josefa had slept was ajar. That surprised me as I always closed it before going out. I closed it securely. Before drifting off to sleep I thought I heard a noise in the street but paid no heed.

Next morning I detected a familiar acrid smell when I went downstairs. Sure enough, Josefa was asleep on our floor. She gave no explanation but merely looked at me with bland, cat-like satisfaction. She had crept into our garden and, finding the back-door closed, had smashed a window to gain entry.

This was too much. Firmly, I ordered her out. She shuffled meekly out into the street, but no further. She squatted against the house wall, unwilling to leave, calling to be allowed back in. That night I heard her wailing outside and scratching at our front door, sounding uncomfortably like an abandoned animal. And then she disappeared, as abruptly as she had come.

But we still felt her presence. For many nights afterwards, at the slightest creak of a door or window, Thea and I would stiffen, wondering if Josefa had returned and whether we would find her in the morning lying once more on our floor.

Weeks later, when we had finally reassured ourselves, a tile shifted in the roof over our heads. We tensed and stared up into the darkness, listening anxiously. Then came the soft pad of paws over tiles. A cat, just a cat.

26

OUT OF THE CHRYSALIS

There they go again. Alien voices drifting up to my roof terrace. They always say the same predictable things, the sort of things that no doubt I said when I first came to the *pueblo*. But that was a long time ago, when every day in the *pueblo* was one of discovery and I was eager to share my newly-acquired local knowledge. I have given up acting as a one-man information bureau. Now I usually take cover when I hear laboured breathing and plaintive queries.

"Why do they make these streets so steep? Why do you think that fellow was taking the donkey into his house? Why do they all wear black? Do you think anything has changed here in a thousand years?"

I peer down at them through the geraniums. Two perfect specimens, huffing and puffing up the street. One in baggy shorts, the other in crotch-hugging hot pants, both in bulging T-shirts and displaying frightening expanses of crimson, sun-damaged flesh.

"Wait, Nigel, here's a lovely spot for a snap. Yes, me and this lovely goat. What do you mean 'Guess which is the wife?' Ha! Ha! Very funny, I'm sure. Oh! You nasty brute! Nigel, look what it's done to my shoes."

Truth to tell, that sort of conversation no longer takes place. The mules that used to be stabled in almost every house have gone and, in the interests of hygiene, goats have been banned from the village streets. Changes have been coming thick and fast, many of them spurred by the influx of tourists. They are arriving in increasing numbers, drifting up from the coast to see "The Real Spain." They don't usually stay too long, but long enough to get up your nose. Some days it is difficult to get out of your front door for the happy snappers blocking the street. Leave the door open a fraction and you are likely to have a living-roomful of strangers, all commenting on the furnishings and videoing the details for posterity.

Ah, the videos! Tour buses have started arriving, disgorging crowds of trippers each with a camera glued to his or her eye. They video everything, balconies, each other, cobbles, flowers, each other again, but especially the few mules that still plod the streets. "Look! A donkey!" they exclaim. No point in explaining that these are not donkeys, which are smaller and less useful as work animals. Four-legged animals possess a strange fascination for visitors. As soon as they see one, smiles spread across their faces as they grope for their cameras, breaking off only to mutter, with unanswerable logic: "Very Spanish here, isn't it?"

The changes crept up almost unobserved at first. Then we woke up one morning and realised that the Costa del Sol, which seemed safely far away, had crept up the valley and was on our doorstep. Sooner or later, of course, it was bound to happen. The *pueblo* has become a tourist sight and soon it will be a tourist resort. For a long time it escaped that fate, but it was too pretty, too close to the coast, to avoid being "discovered." Cash has poured in from foreign and Spanish visitors eager to have their holiday home in the sun.

Half the old quarter has been sold, the other half is up for sale. Families are glad to offload ancient dwellings with uneven floors and beamed ceilings to move to new apartments that have been constructed at the modern end of the *pueblo*. They may have echo-chamber characteristics but they are where the action is, the new shops, the disco, neon-lit pubs. The Street of Bitterness is becoming the Street of Ghosts, as the neighbours move out. Many houses lie empty for most of the year, only briefly coming alive when their new owners visit. The growth industry in the old quarter is in souvenir shops; they sprout like vine shoots.

A new highway encourages more and more tour buses to make the climb from the coast and the soporific clip-clop of mules and donkeys passing through the narrow streets has been replaced by another sound, the angry roar of shiny new cars and swarming motor-cycles. Interspersed with that is the sound of suitcases being trundled along on wheels by arriving and departing holidaymakers who have rented village houses.

In the old days, my neighbours' terraces were rarely used except for hanging out washing or for an interchange of gossip over the rooftops. Now I step out of an evening and hear a babble of voices in half a dozen languages. These new neighbours, enchanted with the balmy climate, use the terraces almost 24 hours a day, for sunbathing, eating, talking, partying until the small hours. Often, after midnight, I think about telling them there are working folk here who need to sleep, but it's hardly worth the trouble—tomorrow they will be gone and a new batch of holidaymakers will arrive.

Out in the *campo*, you need eyes in the back of your head to avoid massive four-wheel-drives rumbling along newly-carved tracks to luxury villas and fields of newly-planted avocadoes, loquats and custard apples. Something called "rural tourism" has taken off. It means that Antonio can do up his derelict *cortijo*, add a swimming pool, let the place at astonishing prices to city sunseekers, and retire to the *pueblo* to count his money.

While youngsters gabble into mobile phones, parabolic anten-nas sprout from terraces and whitewashed walls, an indigestible addition to the village's Moorish-style architecture. Instead of going out and talking their heads off while getting totally pie-eyed, the neighbours have become just like the folk in darkest suburbia, hypno-tised by the latest video film as they recline on plastic sofas. A local television station screens endless re-runs of every *fiesta* and—after mid-night—pornographic films. The social fabric is being rewoven; or is it coming apart at the seams?

The drug scourge that has swept the country has also affected the *pueblo*. Teenagers smoke hashish and heroin infiltrates even the

Barrio Alto. No longer—the saddest comment of all—do the villagers leave their doors unlocked.

"They're ruining the place!" mutter the old hands, aghast at the invasion of their bolthole, wondering where it will all end. Nothing can be more calculated to provoke the wrath of the villagers, although they're usually too polite to make a retort. However, one day after listening to a half hour of this sort of stuff, Miguel exploded.

"Spoiling the *pueblo*? *Cojones*! What a load of *mierda* (shit). As far as I'm concerned, what's happening is de *puta madre*!"

The expression de *puta madre* did not mean, as you might guess from a literal translation, that my or anybody else's mother was a whore. It was Miguel's way of indicating extreme approbation. He had a colourful vocabulary of expletives. "*Yo cago en Dios*" (I shit on God) was one of them and he used it now.

"*Yo cago en Dios*! These are the best years we have had! What's so clever about carrying water from the well and cooking on a wood stove? What's so special about whitewash and wooden beams? I had that all my childhood. Now I want fitted carpets and a flush toilet and television and comfort, just like everybody else! Don't tell me about doing everything by hand. What's so clever about that? And what was so romantic about the old ways. My father worked like a slave all his life, ploughing, planting, cutting timber in the mountains. It wore him out. He was just a shadow in the end. And all he earned was a handful of pesetas."

He was right enough. The *pueblo* has never had it so good. It's their turn to be obsessed with materialist values, just like anywhere else, and it probably marks not a change in sentiment but in opportunity. In the past, what romantic outsiders saw as contentment and satisfaction was often nothing less than resignation. The yearning was there all the time.

The poverty and bitter memories were masked by the good humour of the people, always ready to crack a joke or launch into song, just as the eternal sunshine blinded the casual visitor to the unhealed scars and continuing injustices. Only the death of the implacable old patriarch finally opened the window to the fresh air and new ideas that have transformed the *pueblo*.

It's not hard to find the physical improvements. When we arrived, the *pueblo* youngsters did not even have a proper football pitch and their impromptu games often ended when the ball flew off into the *barranco*. Today they can compete at everything from karate to basketball. In summer their screams echo around a municipal swimming pool and broad-beamed mothers attend swimming classes, though not their husbands, apparently reluctant to expose their bellies to possible ridicule from contemporaries.

Unimaginable education facilities have been installed in a place where only the children of *los ricos* could hope to reach university. Now parents who have never managed to write more than their names proudly encourage their children to graduate from university. Reading has never been a popular Spanish pastime, but at least the *pueblo* now has a well-stocked library. In the evenings, a gaggle of schoolchildren troops in to study, consult the books, and whisper to one another at the tops of their voices, impervious to the librarian's calls for silence.

Never have the young had such freedom. They make excursions to Madrid and talk of Europe as though they were a part of it. Today's teenagers are taller and plumper than their parents. They eat more meat, more dairy foods, and gulp down a frightening assortment of gooey cakes. Although it's a richer, tastier diet than bread smeared with olive oil, chick peas, lentils, potatoes and salted fish, which is what the old folk were reared on, it is not a healthier one. The old-timers were as lean and sinewy as bamboo canes, but they did not suffer from heart problems as do an increasing number of the hamburger generation.

Fortunately, these days the odds on surviving a heart attack are considerably higher than in the past when ailing villagers were bundled into a taxi for a marathon trip to hospital. There's an ambulance service and a new hospital has been built within half-an-hour's drive. There are a lot more teeth about, too. Once the only cure for a rotten molar was extraction, usually without any anaesthetic. "I did clean my teeth once, when I was 10. But after that it seemed too much trouble," admitted one friend, who at 60 had finally acquired a set of false teeth. For his sons it's a different story, as trained dentists have replaced the tooth-pullers.

The stately old ways of courtship are gone. Wordless encounters in the cacophonous village disco have replaced the whisperings and sighs through the *rejas*. New blood enters the *pueblo* as the boys zoom off on their motorcycles to chase girls in other villages. Following the new liberal trends, a number of couples have set up house together without the blessings of the church, but pregnancy still usually leads to a marriage in white and a full church service. That's the way it has always been, for pregnant teenagers are nothing new to the *pueblo*. How they became pregnant with all the chaperones and tight security of the past is one of life's mysteries. The difference today is that newly-weds honeymoon in the Canaries or the Caribbean—Cancún is the favourite. In the past they generally stayed with relatives and often mother came, too. However, the happy couple is still expected to spend a large chunk of their savings on buying presents to be delivered to every relative and friend on their return from their brief romantic idyll.

Rigid codes are bending or have vanished altogether. Not that everything has changed. Old ways die hard in the *pueblo*. Mother's place is still in the home, cooking, scouring, washing, looking after the children. Pushing a pram along the main street remains an exercise only for the young father most confident of his masculinity. While the old generation continues in near-perpetual mourning, however, the tradition is losing force. Young women have rebelled and even their mothers are discarding black, after the ritual few months following a relative's death, and adopting the latest fashions.

People in general rejoice at the revolution in their lives. The *pueblo* has become a livelier, more prosperous place than anybody could have imagined when poverty truly dressed it in mourning. In the Barrio Alto old men look bemused as they sit in their doorways to catch the morning sun. No wonder they have a stunned air. It has all happened so fast. Soon they will be gone and their houses, too, will be up for sale.

It is hard to argue against change, even for we nostalgics, when you see what it has done for El Chico, our neighbour with the devilish grin. El Chico never had any schooling. His family were ashamed of his backwardness and could not bear to send him away for special tuition, even if it had been available and they could have afforded it. Instead they gratefully accepted the state subsidy for the retarded and protected El Chico like a baby. His mother did everything for him, even tying his shoe laces. He wandered the *pueblo*, inoffensive but apparently beyond help, the butt of pranksters and the terror of visitors.

Then his mother died and, like Spain after the Caudillo's departure, he emerged from his chrysalis. He has gone to a special college, where they have taught him to dress himself and to do simple jobs. He comes back to the *pueblo* for holidays, spruced up, bright-eyed, with a new pride. Maybe eventually, 40 years late, El Chico will even learn to speak.

27

BUTTERFLIES IN THE *PUEBLO*

That spring morning when we left the *pueblo* and walked into the hills for a feast with Antonio and his family was not that long ago but it seems like a dream from another century. In fact, it was in another century. More than 30 years ago have passed since we tramped up the narrow track, past tumbledown farmhouses and vine-covered hillsides.

At the *cortijo* we feasted on stewed kid, then—steeped in garlic and Moscatel wine—dreamed through the long, thyme-scented, cicada-buzzing, heat-hazy afternoon. Thirty years have flown by since that homeward journey when Paquito turned from chasing a rainbow swirl of butterflies to fix solemn eyes on me and ask with an innocence that can never be repeated: "Are there butterflies in **your *pueblo*?**" I don't recall my answer. All I remember is a day burnished by nostalgia to a golden perfection.

There are still butterflies in the *pueblo* but the years have fled and so, too, has Paquito. The *pueblo* is a different place now. No longer does the crack of hoof on cobble serve as a morning alarm; men go out to the country now on motorcycles and in four-wheel-drives. No longer is bread delivered from panniers on a mule's back; the bakers have sold their animals. No longer does Manolo bellow "*Pescado! Muy barato!*" as he pushes his barrow through the streets. The music of a hundred goats' hoofs, followed by the limping steps of the old goatherd, is no longer heard outside our door. Tourism rather than agriculture is what most villagers live off. The *pueblo* has entered the 21st century.

Newcomers continue to arrive seeking the simple life, of course. But their idea of "simple" is a little different from ours all those years ago. Now it embraces hot showers, flush toilets, swimming pools, satellite TV, Internet connection, credit cards and designer clothes. Inexplicably, *garbanzos* don't seem to get a look-in.

But some things do not change. The mornings are still pungent with strong coffee and frying *churros* and the nights perfumed by jasmin. It can still take an hour to buy an egg in a village shop while housewives debate the latest doings of their neighbours. Recognising their value, perhaps unconsciously, the village clings to its rituals and celebrates its *fiestas* as enthusiastically as ever.

Mobile phones are silenced, miraculously if briefly, in Holy Week as the shuffling of feet and the smack of wooden staves against cobbles mark the progress of the images through darkened streets. Every January the Three Kings continue to receive their usual ecstatic welcome from the children—although now they may arrive in the village not by mule but by helicopter.

The *sierras* watch over the flock of village houses just as they always have, the Mediterranean reflects the same brilliant light, the ancient rituals mark the seasons, the swifts arrive, summer swelters, the grapes ripen, the rains renew. And, as always, every June a rocket sailing into the heavens signals the start of the *feria*. As the village band strikes up, it's impossible not to feel a surge of emotion as you are reminded once more that—come what may—the *pueblo* endures.